What the Bible REALLY Teaches

Marriage
Restoration
Divorce
Confusion
Healing
Rejection
Remarriage
Conversion

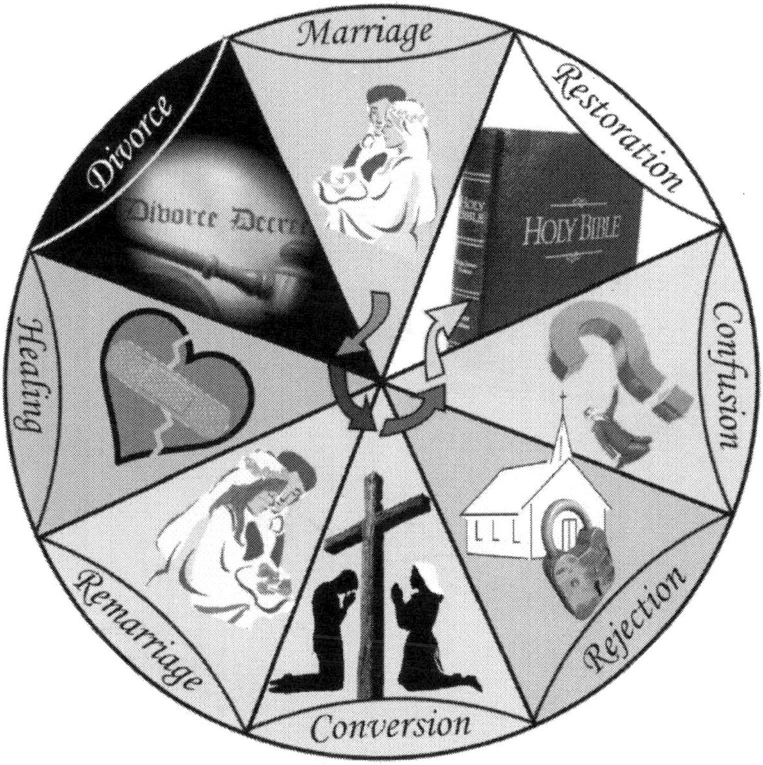

About Divorce And Remarriage

Should The Church Accept New Converts With Divorce and Remarriage In Their Past?

Mark Bullen

This is not your typical, superficial study on the issue of divorce and remarriage. *Mark Bullen* has taken the time and effort to thoroughly delve into this controversial matter, not because the subject directly affects him, he and his wife were pure on their wedding day and have remained faithful for over 23 years. Rather, he has broached this issue because his heart is set firmly on the path of Truth. Mark has not approached the difficulties of this topic from a denominational bias, or to bring the Scriptures into subjection to an emotional position, but has sought, just as the title purports, to truly determine *"What the Bible Really Teaches About Divorce and Remarriage"*. I challenge you to get your *Bible*, like a good Berean and lay it beside this book to see whether these things be so. Is your own position on the matter based on Scripture or a failure to properly Apprehend Truth?

~ ***J L Wallace***, *ApprehendingTruth.net*

Divorce and remarriage is an area of intense controversy among Christians. It is admittedly a difficult and complex issue. In his book, *"What the Bible Really Teaches About Divorce and Remarriage"*, author and pastor *Mark Bullen* takes an exhaustive approach in establishing a decidedly Biblical, yet understandable view of the subject. Rather than undergird or echo a traditionalist position, *Mark* seeks to unveil exactly what God communicates via His Word. I am convinced, through his study, he has arrived at conclusions which reflect the spirit and letter of Scripture regarding this often volatile topic.

~***Britt Williams***, *pastor - Consuming Fire Christian Fellowship, Gloster, Mississippi*

It seems almost inevitable that the pursuit of the truth of God's Word and the desire to live it out will lead you down one of just a few possible paths of church fellowship. If there was a divorce and remarriage in your past, or your spouses, those paths will often run you into a wall that has been disguised as truth. This book exposes the false doctrine of divorce fixing divorce and reveals the truth of what God says about divorce and His heart toward it from the Old Testament to the New Testament.

The truth that this book brings to light saved my marriage!

~**Randall Tarrant**, Brookfield, Missouri

The church is facing a time where confusion abounds and the enemy is attacking on many fronts, primarily in the area of holiness. In the midst of this trial there are some finding their way through the confusion, hanging on to the Word of God, and seeking the narrow way. Inevitably, during their quest there comes a time when the issue of marriage, specifically divorce and remarriage, becomes a matter of consideration, and rightly so as these things are indeed precious to God. It is with great hope that those beginning this journey, as well as those well on their way, would consider these things afresh in the light of the Scriptures with the help of this book! This book provides a clear, fresh study of the Word of God, reflecting back on church history, to provide the reader with a clear understanding of the heart of God in these matters.

~ *David Benoit*, *Gasport, New York*

What the Bible Really Teaches

About Divorce And Remarriage

Should The Church Accept New Converts
With Divorce and Remarriage In Their Past?

by

Mark Bullen

Living Faith Books
Brookfield, Missouri

What The Bible Really Teaches About Divorce and
Remarriage

ISBN-13: 978-0615627250
ISBN-10: 0615627250

Living Faith Books is an imprint of:
Apprehending Truth Publishers
PO Box 249
Brookfield, Missouri 64628

Apprehending Truth Publishers
http://www.ApprehendingTruth.net

What The Bible Really Teaches About Divorce and Remarriage

Mark Bullen

Contents

Sixth Edition

2012

What the Bible Really Teaches About Divorce And Remarriage

Should The Church Accept New Converts With Divorce and Remarriage In Their Past?

Preface

I am a busy father supporting my lovely wife and eleven precious children. We run a roofing business, a dairy, and I pastor a growing church. I have little time to spare; but felt this book was a must. This book is written to set the record straight and defend those victimized by false doctrine — I mean those repentant seekers who are devastated when told that, because they have divorce and remarriage in their past, they cannot be a part of the body of Christ; unless they break up their homes. After years of study and research to find the truth for my own conscience and faith, I have ventured to put my findings in writing in hopes of salvaging as many of these victims as possible. I have no past to hide or justify as a motivation; but am thankful that, by God's grace, my wife and I were both pure on our wedding day, and have only known each other.

Striving for biblical accuracy has a way of leaving one without many friends, but if Noah had not been concerned about "contending for the faith once delivered" in his day, he would not have made it on the ark with his family. He was left out of every

3

religious group of his day, but God doesn't see as man sees. With this confidence, I have written what I believe to be the position of the apostolic church on the subject of divorce and remarriage. I am fallible, and you can decide for yourself after you have fully considered the evidence presented. If you don't agree, at least maybe you will be more understanding of us who disagree with you. I am striving to be honest with the Word. Jesus said, "Blessed are the merciful, for they shall obtain mercy." I fear that too often we, who don't have a past to deal with, don't want to dirty our hands with those who do. I think many times this becomes incorporated into our doctrine. In our zeal to keep our church clean, we forget to be merciful, and become more rigid than even the apostles of Christ. We begin to call something sin that God doesn't call sin; or fail to forgive what God has forgiven. Sometimes we are all too happy to let some other church deal with these people. We end up with a doctrinal stance full of absurdities, because it is not Bible doctrine. My prayer is that those with a past will be dealt with as Jesus and the apostles would have dealt with them; and therefore can find that the Great Physician always has a cure for those willing to follow the prescription.

In the 2011 update you will find I have altered my view of this issue slightly. I have realized that my view of God's inspired Word was not what it should have been; and now I see that if we truly believe that "all Scripture is inspired by God", then we can't be toying with the idea that Jesus corrected Moses. I didn't think I was doing this, but now realize I was to some degree. I am convinced that Jesus is vindicating God's Law by teaching it in its true light. I am convinced that

Jesus' words are in harmony with all the other Scriptures that were inspired by Him. This may sound obvious, but this is where the root problem is in discerning the divorce and remarriage issue. As you read, you will understand clearer what I am saying; and what I have changed. **If you don't believe that the Bible, including Moses' Law, always prescribes what is the very best thing to do under the circumstances, then you don't believe the Bible is God's Holy Inspired Word.**

Brief Summary Of Our Position:

For those without the time or patience to hear the entire matter step by step, I have below a summary of the foundational reasons why I believe what I believe.

1. You cannot properly interpret the Word of God until you understand the relationship of the Old Covenant to the New Covenant.

a. The Ceremonial Law was fulfilled and lost it's relevance by being fulfilled. It was the middle wall of partition between Jew and Gentile (Eph.2:14), and was done away.

b. The Moral Law, which is also called the "righteousness of the law" was not done away; but was written on the hearts of New Covenant believers as the basis of the New Covenant (Heb. 8:10, 10:16). The only way a moral precept can be fulfilled, is by being obeyed; and it never loses its relevance unless God changes His morality. Those under the

5

New Covenant who walk in the Spirit fulfill the righteousness of the Law (Romans 8:4).

c. The Bible is a progressive revelation, but not contradictory. If Jesus had taught contrary to Moses' Law, it would have only proved him a false prophet.

2. Jesus is the Word made flesh. He inspired Moses' Law, and everything He taught was consistent with the Old Testament. He did not "correct Moses", but defended him. He clarified the Law, and interpreted it properly. All that the New Testament teaches on marriage, divorce, and remarriage is consistent with the "righteousness of the Law". Jesus' exception clause must have been the same as Moses' exception clause; unless we believe Jesus changed His mind, because Jesus is the author of Moses' exception clause. The apostle's believed the righteousness of the Law was still relevant. This will be explained further in the study.

3. The doctrine of the church today must be consistent with what Christ and the apostles taught in the first century, or it is heresy. We will illustrate and explain this.

4. Jesus is fulfilling Malachi 3:1-5, and adultery must be defined consistent with Moses' Law (Malachi 4:4).

5. Historically, Biblical Christians have held our view.

1

Larry & Linda

(These fictitious names represent many real people, but this story is one I dealt with personally)

As a young woman Linda fell in love with a man whom she assumed would be her husband for life. Being both unbelievers, they had not much to build a marriage upon. They both started out with good intentions, but Satan's temptations overcame the man, and eventually he gave himself up to fornication. He divorced Linda and continued a life of fornication.

Naturally Linda was broken and devastated. She struggled on in life with an indescribable empty and bitter hole in her heart. After a couple years of healing emotionally, she met Larry, who seemed to be a stable and sincere individual. Larry had never been married, and was willing to overlook Linda's stormy past. They were eventually married with fresh high hopes of having a happy family.

Eventually Larry and Linda had eight children, began

attending a church, professed Christ, and tried to raise their family for the Lord. As they grew in grace, they began to seek a church with higher standards of godliness for the sake of the children and from personal conviction. They struggled to stand alone and do what was right. Linda learned about modest apparel and head covering, and was happy to obey.

Then it happened. As they sought fellowship with a conservative church they were informed of the church's stand on divorce and remarriage. They were told that since Linda's first husband was still alive, she was actually still married to him. Her marriage to Larry was just an adulterous affair. Their children were then illegitimate, and they must separate in order to enter the church as members.

According to the church's beliefs, she should divorce Larry and try to remarry her unbelieving, whoremonger, first husband. If that didn't work, she had to remain single. The children, who were being homeschooled by their "keeper at home" mother, would now have to be put in public school and daycare, so the mother could support the family if Larry's child support wasn't enough, or if he became overwhelmed and disappeared.

Larry, who was said to be living in fornication with Linda, and was therefore never really married, is said to be free to marry a virgin after leaving Linda. Larry could no longer live with his family and bring up his children in the nurture and admonition of the Lord. The church actually expected them to live in separate houses (though they had struggled to pay for one dwelling); still attend the church services and pass the children back and forth; but could no longer be a family until Linda's first husband died.

Had Linda been a harlot and just shacked up with her first husband instead of marrying him like a moral girl would, she could now keep Larry and be in good standing in the church. Had Larry obeyed the church and left Linda; technically he could have married a virgin, started a new family and been considered the "husband of one wife".

ALL THIS, BECAUSE JESUS SUPPOSEDLY "IMPROVED" THE LAW OF THE OLD TESTAMENT???

It is vital to the pure interpretation of Scripture that we find our beliefs in the First Century Apostolic Church. What we preach today must have been a working practice in the first century. If it wouldn't fit there, we dare not teach it today. If you miss this principle for Bible interpretation, you have really missed something important. My concern is to know God's original intent. This can only be found by interpreting Scripture according to its historical setting. We are seeking the faith once for all delivered to the saints. There are a number of basic principles of Bible interpretation that are violated, ignored, and trampled in order to arrive at the position of "no divorce, no remarriage - never".

Well, let's set Larry and Linda as a Jewish couple in the first century, and see how this so called "improvement" actually would have worked - if it were true. For the sake of thinking our theology back to the first century; if we pretend that Jesus' statements about marriage were stated on January

9

3rd at 5 PM, 31 A.D.; then we can establish the following scenario:

STAGE 1: 31 A.D. 4 PM Jan. 3rd. Capernaum:

Linda: She was put away by a writing of divorcement and remarried according to Moses' Law. Now, according to God's inspired Law (The first five books of the Bible, the books of Moses):

· Is she breaking the seventh commandment? No.

· Is she truly married? Yes.

· Is she an adulteress? No.

· Is she living in sin? No.

· Is she bound by the Law to the second man? Yes.

· Is she still bound by the Law to the first man? No.

· Should she get a divorce? No.

· Should she go back to the first husband? No, it is strictly forbidden as an abomination.

· What would God have her to do? Ask forgiveness for her part of the failure to the first marriage, and now strive to be the godliest wife possible in the second marriage.

· What would happen if she were considered an adulteress? She would be stoned.

Larry: If he (as a virgin man) married Linda after she had been put away by her first husband; or if he put away his first wife for whoredom, and later married Linda:

Now, according to God's revelation to man:

· Is he breaking the seventh commandment? No.

· Is he an adulterer? No.

· Is he truly married? Yes.

· Is he living in sin? No.

· Should he get divorced? No.

· Should he go back to the first wife? Absolutely not.

· What is the righteous thing for him to do? He should stay married and strive not to repeat the mistakes of the past which have been confessed and forsaken.

STAGE 2: 31 A.D. 5 PM Jan. 3rd. Jerusalem

Jesus is asked by the Pharisees if it is lawful to put away your wife for "every cause" (This was a controversy among the Jews). Jesus answers with a question: What did Moses command you? They answer that Moses allowed them to give a bill of divorce and put away their wives (referring to Deut. 24). Jesus answers that Moses allowed divorce for "some uncleanness" because of the hardness of their hearts, but from the beginning this (Deut 24) was not the case. Jesus takes them back to Genesis (also written by Moses), "Have ye not read, that he which made them in the beginning made them male and female, and said, For this cause shall a man leave father and mother, and shall cleave to his wife: and they twain shall be one flesh? Wherefore they are no more twain, but one flesh. What therefore God hath joined together, let not man put asunder." We should always read everything on the subject, not just the part we like - as did the Jews.

Then Jesus went on to say, "And I say unto you, Whosoever shall put away his wife, except it be for fornication, and shall marry another, committeth adultery; and whoso marrieth her which is put away doth commit adultery." This statement was backing up the original intent of God's Inspired Law through Moses - not correcting it; but since some interpret that Jesus changed the law, and now allowed no divorce or remarriage as in the "espousal theory"; let's see how this would work:

STAGE 3: 31 A.D. 7 PM Jan. 3rd. Capernaum:

Linda: Now that Jesus made that statement, according to those who believe Larry and Linda should divorce...The Espousal Theory:

· Is she breaking the seventh commandment? Yes.

· Is she an adulteress? Yes.

· Is she married? No.

· Is she living in sin? Yes.

· Should she divorce? Yes.

· Is she bound by the Law to the second man? No.

· Should she go back to the first? Yes.

Larry: Now, according to the same theory:

· Is he breaking the seventh commandment? Yes.

· Is he married? No.

· Is he living in sin? Yes.

· Can he raise his children and lead his home? No.

· Should he divorce and try to get the first harlot back? Yes.

■ IS THIS WHAT JESUS WAS DOING?

Don't you realize that what you teach today had to also be taught and practiced by the apostles in the first century? So how did they reconcile these gross errors that this doctrine creates?

This mysterious "line in the sand" that people try to draw between the New and Old Testaments is simply not there. The transition was very slight as can be seen in Acts 15 and 21. God opened the door for Gentiles to be church members without becoming Jewish proselytes twelve years after Pentecost (Acts 10-11), where we find Peter still preaching to "Jews only" and obeying Mosaic dietary laws. For the first twelve years after Pentecost, Moses' Law and Circumcision were the church standard — requirements for membership and baptism - No Gentile could be baptized unless he was a Jewish proselyte for the first twelve years after Pentecost. The Apostles had to have a conference in Acts 15 to confirm that the Gentiles need not be circumcised and obey Moses' Law to be saved — Twenty years after

13

Pentecost! Jesus didn't make drastic changes, but taught the "spirit" and "righteousness" of the law. The "righteousness of the Law" is to be fulfilled in believers who walk after the same Spirit that inspired God's Law (Rom. 8:4). God is writing His moral Law on our hearts as the primary aspect of the new covenant for life in Messiah's Kingdom (Heb 8:10). Twenty Nine years after Pentecost we find Paul and James speaking in Acts 21, where we learn that Paul never taught Jews to forsake Moses or circumcision; that Paul himself kept the Law; and that there were thousands of Jews who were believers and zealous of Moses' Law — Maybe you've been taught wrong concerning the transition from Old Testament to New Testament. It was only the ceremonial law that was done away as the middle wall of partition between Jew and Gentile (Eph. 2). The Law was changed to allow for a new priesthood, a new covenant, a heavenly temple or tabernacle, etc.; but the morality of God's Law is the morality of God, and He hasn't changed.

In 1 Cor. 7 Paul tells us that the wife is bound by the Law; but this can only mean that the Law's teachings concerning marriage were still relevant and binding on New Testament saints. In Romans 7 Paul "speaks to them that know the Law" and speaks about marriage as an illustration – once again showing that the Law was still relevant concerning marriage in Paul's mind.

Some will say remarried couples were "grandfathered in" in the first century; but this can only mean that we should do the same for new converts today. Others will say they weren't in trouble until they heard the new teaching. OK, so where do we see the apostles splitting up remarried Jews and Gentiles? Those who teach "no divorce, no remarriage under any circumstance" avoid taking their doctrine back to the first century and trying to reconcile it with the obvious problems it creates. This is a very strong argument against any doctrine. **There is not one trace of the policy of demanding "divorce before baptism" in the New Testament or early church writings due to remarriage.**

Did Jesus draw a line in history where remarried people were suddenly unmarried adulterers? Where legitimate children suddenly became illegitimate? Where fathers suddenly became "live ins"? ...or not?

■ HOW DOES THIS FIT WITH MATTHEW 23:1-4?

"Then spake Jesus to the multitude, and to his disciples, saying, The scribes and the Pharisees sit in Moses' seat: All therefore whatsoever they bid you observe, that observe and do; but do not ye after their works: for they say, and do not."

Jesus makes it clear here and many other places that he didn't come to "correct" Moses, but to defend and fulfill the Law. If Jesus had started teaching contrary to God's Word, it would have only proved him to be a false prophet. Jesus worked to clear up misconceptions about God's Law, but never to change His own Word. In Luke 16 he has Abraham telling the rich man in hell concerning the salvation of his brethren: *"They have Moses and the prophets, let them hear them."* "Moses and the Prophets" was God's inspired Word -- inspired by Jesus himself - the Word made flesh. Jesus himself stated in John 10 that the "Scriptures cannot be broken" – they cannot be set aside, but stand firm, and we must bow to them, not the other way around.   Listen to Jesus' words:

Matthew 5:17 Think not that I am come to destroy the law, or the prophets: I am not come to destroy, but to fulfill. 18 For verily I say unto you, Till heaven and earth pass, one jot or one tittle shall in no wise pass from the law, till all be fulfilled. 19 Whosoever therefore shall break one of these least commandments, and shall teach men so, he shall be called the least in the kingdom of heaven: but whosoever shall do and teach them, the same shall be called great in the kingdom of heaven. 20 For I say unto you, That except your righteousness shall exceed the righteousness of the scribes and Pharisees, ye shall in no case enter into the kingdom of heaven.

- Exceeding the Pharisees' righteousness is living by the "spirit" or "intent" of the Law of God from the heart, not hiding your sin behind your abuse of the "letter" of the law. Through the rest of the Sermon on the Mount Jesus is comparing what the Pharisees lived with what God's Law actually taught. This is important to remember.

What if the apostles had started preaching that remarried Jews under Moses' Law were not even married; had bastard children; should divorce and commit the abomination of going back to the first? Wouldn't we have heard about it? You know we would. This would have been a greater concern to the Jews than to people today. Did Jesus or the apostles ever demand divorce before baptism? If Paul preached "repent, and turn to God"; would remarried Jews think he meant for them to break up their homes and live single? Get acquainted with history before jumping to a conclusion that destroys homes and can tragically stumble seeking souls!

Would a Jewish man or woman believe that to enter the Messiah's Kingdom they must now do what was unrighteous and an abomination to God an hour ago? If the apostles didn't divide Jewish homes, did they divide Gentile homes in the same remarried state? If God not only forgave, but allowed divorce and remarriage under certain conditions among His own covenant people because they had "hard hearts" in their fallen state; would he not pardon Gentiles coming to Christ with divorce and remarriage in their past when they had less teaching and harder hearts than his own covenant people? If in the first century, what about today? These questions must be answered with Scripture in historical accuracy before one can set aside our appeal with a clear conscience before God.

■ DAVID AND BECKY

Another true scenario with fictitious names will illustrate the problems we get into by forcing the Bible to teach what we want instead of searching for simple truth.

David and Becky are married and attending a church that believes the espousal theory about divorce and remarriage in the New Testament (which will be explained later). David forsakes the faith, turns to adultery, and wants to divorce Becky. Since she has been taught that she cannot divorce or consent to divorce under any circumstance, she refuses to sign the papers to release David. The Law at the time didn't allow David to divorce Becky without sufficient cause, so he could never obtain a divorce. The result of not letting the unbeliever depart, as the Bible commands, is as follows. David would go out and live in sin for a while; but whenever he wanted to come home and sleep with Becky, he was free to do so. She was commanded to "render due benevolence" to her husband, which he still was; so she became a part of three way relations with this man. He was allowed to set this example for the children, and give Becky whatever disease he may have gotten while he was out. She became expecting during his stays at home. The children's hopes were raised and then shattered once again. It seemed the church and God had no functional solution to this problem.

Isn't it something that God's Word can be so grossly ignored when it clearly says, **"But if the unbelieving depart, let him depart. A brother or a sister is not under bondage in such cases: but God hath called us to peace." (I Cor. 7:15)** God hath called us to what? PEACE.

Is there an alternative interpretation that fits the first century as well as today? Is there an alternative interpretation that creates peace and sanity, rather than chaos and confusion? Is there a Bible teaching on divorce and remarriage that doesn't leave you with absurdities and contradictions? I believe there is! The

Great Physician doesn't leave us without practical, workable solutions. When the Bible is interpreted consistent with principles of truth, historical accuracy, and honesty, a different picture emerges.

No doubt, this is an emotionally charged subject, full of different biases and fears. Some people are full of fears about this subject, and would rather just trash the whole issue, and those involved. A church leader once said to me, "If we opened that door (of accepting remarried couples) do you realize what kind of people we might allow in?" Charity demands we dig for the apostolic position and follow it. Our character may be attacked for doing so, but that is part of walking in the footsteps of Jesus. We must not fear doing things God's way, but must trust that he knows what is best. When reaching the lost, you will get a Simon Magus now and then, but so did the apostles.

My wife and I were pure on our marriage day. We didn't hold hands until we were engaged to be married; and we didn't kiss until the preacher said, "You may kiss the bride". So understand I am not fighting for some personal agenda; but my concern is Biblical accuracy and the welfare of sincere seeking souls. I would not have studied and written this book had churches just allowed these repentant remarried people in; but their reasons for keeping them out were so inconsistent that I had to know the truth. At present my family cannot enjoy the luxury of being in "the crowd" or a "mainstream" due to our position. It is a sacrifice to fight for accuracy; and all those who agree with this book, yet stay in a group that doesn't agree just for the benefits of a larger group ought to be ashamed of themselves.

19

The main question is: "Is it lawful to divorce if your mate breaks wedlock by immorality? And if divorced lawfully (no longer under obligation to reconcile), is it then lawful to remarry?" We believe the Apostolic Church said, Yes. We know the Anabaptists said, Yes. We know the Mennonites until around 1800 said, Yes. We know the protestant churches said, Yes. And, we know the Roman Catholics said, No - but evidently after the tenth century. There were individual writers who believed remarriage was wrong, even when divorce was right; yet these also believed it was wrong for a widow to marry again as well as other obvious errors. There has been the same presumption placed on the early church writings as has been placed on Jesus' words. Justin Martyr, for example states, "...all who, by human law, are twice married, are in the eyes of our Master sinners, and those who look upon a woman to lust after her." It is amazing how everyone assumes "human law" is the same as "God's Law" – they thus assume Justin is on their side.

God says in the book of **Malachi 3: 5** *And I will come near to you to judgment; and I will be a swift witness against the sorcerers, and against the adulterers, and against false swearers, and against those that oppress the hireling in his wages, the widow, and the fatherless, and that turn aside the stranger from his right, and fear not me, saith the LORD of hosts. 6 For I am the LORD, I change not; therefore ye sons of Jacob are not consumed.*

When Jesus came He did preach against the adulterers and false swearers, etc. in His Sermon On The Mount; but His teaching was against those who abused God's Law, not those who followed it. God states that He doesn't change, and the last command in Malachi before the 400 years of silence preceding John the Baptist was:

> **Malachi 4:4** *"Remember ye the law of Moses my servant, which I commanded unto him in Horeb for all Israel, with the statutes and judgments."*

If allowing divorce and remarriage according to God's Law is adultery, as some claim, then God told them to keep doing it for 400 more years until Jesus would come and correct the Law of God!? Can you accept such poor use of the Word of God? Jesus is The Word in the flesh – He didn't come to correct God's Word. What Jesus states is a general rule against those that were abusing Deut. 24.

The stating of a general rule without also stating all the exceptions does not necessarily mean that there are no exceptions; and it is foolish to assume there are no exceptions, just because they are not stated every time the general rule is stated. This happens often in Scripture. Just ask yourself if the following commands have exceptions, and ask yourself why these exceptions don't have to always be mentioned every time the general rule is mentioned, and you will get the idea:

1. **1Pe 2:13 Submit yourselves to every ordinance of man for the Lord's sake: whether it be to the king, as supreme; Or unto governors,...**
2. **Heb 13:17 Obey them that have the rule over you, and submit yourselves:...**
3. **Col 3:22 Servants, obey in all things your masters according to the flesh;**

4. **Col 3:20 Children, obey your parents in all things:**
5. **Eph 5:22 Wives, submit yourselves unto your own husbands, as unto the Lord.**

Jesus actually gave the same exception as Moses did – Why would you expect anything else? Who inspired Moses? Jesus simply labeled the abuse of the Law's allowance for divorce "adultery".

We are presenting to you basically the same position that we believe the Apostolic Church had; the one we believe the Ana-Baptists had; and the one the Mennonites evidently held until around the 1800's. This "no divorce, no remarriage" stance evidently came from Romanists. It stems from their erroneous beliefs about marriage and celibacy.

2

Whom Do We Trust?

"Now the Spirit speaketh expressly, that in the latter times some shall depart from the faith, giving heed to seducing spirits, and doctrines of devils; speaking lies in hypocrisy; having their conscience seared with a hot iron; forbidding to marry, and commanding to abstain from meats, which God hath created to be received with thanksgiving of them which believe and know the truth" I Tim. 4:1-3

It is important in this study to understand the "trends" that followed first century apostolic Christianity. There were those who "turned the grace of God into lasciviousness" (Jude 4); and there were those who went the other direction into forced asceticism. (I Tim. 4:1-3; Col. 2:14-23). There have always been radicals on both sides with their arguments. The challenge of the servant of God, who seeks to contend for the "faith once delivered to the saints", is to steer between the rocks and ditches of error. It is not a little matter to do this, but with a "single eye" we can

23

become full of light. Most people who end up in error do so from an "evil eye" (double motive). They are building on false principles to defend their "ism".

Even though the early church became, at times and in certain places, over zealous about virginity and self denial, to the point of later generations establishing forced celibacy and monasteries; <u>yet there is no trace of them demanding converts to divorce from second marriages before baptism.</u>   The early writings were usually individuals sharing their opinions, and were not official church teaching, which represented the universal doctrine of the day. The reason we don't see "divorce before baptism" taught is because they believed that "Life begins at conversion".   Often they are stating a general rule, and people assume they are teaching something they are not.   In the zeal of fighting flesh and intemperance; they sometimes forgot God's provisions for: "What to do when sin happens, the ideal is not met, or when people are in a vulnerable position." Our pride, too often, doesn't want to allow for those without the gift of singleness, or the converts with a past.

The people who hold the absolute "no divorce, no remarriage" position, are usually very sincere and well meaning people.   Some really believe they are contending for right doctrine; but have not been well informed. They have trusted their denomination to teach them correctly, and have not double checked their position. We do not intend to make them out as devils and deceivers; but cannot follow their error.

■ THE ESPOUSAL THEORY

The teaching that would have split up Larry and Linda; and wouldn't let Becky grant David a divorce in chapter one; is what we are calling the espousal theory. Those who hold this teaching say the "exception clause" (except for fornication), in Matthew 5:32 and 19:9 only refers to one situation: That if you find your espoused bride has been unfaithful, you can put her away (which required a divorce in Jewish custom), and marry another. They say that this alone is the only circumstance where you can divorce and remarry without committing adultery. One thing they usually overlook is that when a Jewish man put away a new bride because she was not a virgin on their wedding night, he had already consummated the marriage and slept with her on the wedding night. In spite of this glaring fact, they say if she goes into sexual sin after the wedding night, you can't divorce and remarry. They believe that Jesus teaches contrary to the Law of Moses (God's inspired Word), does away with what the law taught about marriage and divorce, and re-established God's original plan for man and woman before the fall as an absolute law, with no exceptions for sin's affects or sinners with a past. They would seem to imply that Moses messed up, and Jesus came to correct him and straighten things out. I cannot accept this because the New Testament declares the Old Testament to be the inspired Word of God; and at the same time declares Jesus to be the Word of God become flesh. NO, Jesus didn't change His mind, and have to come and correct His own Word. The Apostles of Christ held the Old Testament Scriptures as the inspired Word of God:

- **2Ti 3:16 All scripture is given by inspiration of God, and is profitable for doctrine, for reproof, for correction, for instruction in righteousness: 17 That the man of God may be perfect, throughly furnished unto all good works.**
- **2Pe 1:21 For the prophecy came not in old time by the will of man: but holy men of God spake as they were moved by the Holy Ghost.**

There is another position, which is very similar to the Espousal Theory, and which also allows no divorce, and no remarriage under any circumstance after marriage. They hold that the exception clause does not refer to an espoused bride (because no early church writing knew anything about this espousal theory); but they contend the exception clause only refers to the divorce, and not the remarriage (which is grammatically impossible in Matt. 19). They actually make Jesus say the exact opposite of what He said. Jesus said, "Whosoever shall put away his wife, *except it be for fornication,* and shall marry another, committeth adultery:" They make Him say, "Whosoever shall put away his wife, *even if it be for fornication,* and shall marry another, committeth adultery:" I am amazed that otherwise sensible people cannot see through this error. The sad truth is that modern Mennonites and others who hold to the "no divorce, no remarriage- never" idea don't seem to care how you arrive at this position, just as long as you arrive there. In their ranks you can find numerous teachings that are very different, and arrive at the same conclusion from many different angles, and they are all OK -- **As long as they arrive at the conclusion that the church does not have to accept remarried couples into their membership.**

Some proceed to say that in the early church they didn't actually divorce, but just separated (which is also false). It is a definite twist of Scripture to try to avoid the obvious reason for the exception clause Jesus stated, which we will go in depth with later.

Throughout this study, we will be referring to what these two positions teach, and helping you to see the error and false assumptions these positions are based upon. They forbid all divorce, and all remarriage on any grounds, and strive to separate those who are remarried as living in adultery. They make no distinction between what happened before salvation or illumination and what happened after one knew better. They believe that Christ's expectations of unregenerate couples are the same as His expectations of those in His Kingdom. They seem to think that the provisions God made for the hard-heartedness of Israel, He would not make for lost Gentiles.

We need to find the truth. Did Jesus teach contrary to Moses' Law in the Sermon on the Mount, or just interpret it properly? Did Jesus prohibit all divorce and remarriage, or just under certain circumstances? What about those who were already remarried at that time? Did Jesus wish them all to go divorce their second wife or husband when he made his statements to the Pharisees? Did Jesus go throughout Israel breaking up remarried couples when He went preaching the Kingdom of God? Absolutely not.

It has grieved me for years that some churches, basing their teaching on such flimsy and questionable foundations, will venture to rob children of a happy

27

home, a wife of her husband, and a husband of his family. They aren't rejecting a rebellious, self-willed, high-minded, heretic; but a repentant, growing, striving, soul; and doing so when they see not one trace of this policy in Scripture or the early church!! Would God not make it SUPER CLEAR if he expected us to rip apart families over this!? Wouldn't Paul have at least made mention of what to do with those in a second marriage in his writings, had it been so important not to allow them in the church? Paul deals with many particulars, such as "When meat is safe to eat" (Romans 14); how to deal with "leaven" in the church (I Cor. 5); when to separate and when to forgive (1&2 Cor.); what to do with widows, mixed marriages, and virgins (I Cor. 7); etc. — Surely he would have given ample instruction about receiving those in a second marriage or when to split up a marriage. But, notwithstanding the importance of the issue, there is not one trace of divorce before baptism in the New Testament or early church writings, except for certain later heretical sects like the Marcionites (who didn't accept even first marriages contracted outside their sect).

Now, I'm not saying God failed us. I'm saying we have been too quick to follow someone's ideas without a thorough investigation of the facts available to us. Let's carefully review these facts; and with an open mind, seeking for truth alone, let's see what things we can "know", and what things we can safely "infer" from what we know.

This study is not to justify the loose dealing with marriage and divorce in our day. We don't want to be in either ditch. The extreme amount of divorce is a symptom, not a cause. We need to deal with the causes (immodesty, dead churches, dry preaching, poor leadership and discipline, weak teaching, dating, TV, radio, bad books, lack of evangelism, poor parental example, poor training of children, women in the work force, feminism etc.); to get rid of the symptoms. If someone has a running nose, we don't plug their nostrils.

I admit, some of the early church writings are radical on asceticism; but when reading them, remember a number of things:

❖ They never deny divorce for sexual sin.

❖ The rules made for Church members, most likely did not affect new converts coming to the church with sin in their past. Examples: In the OT if one who was an Israelite was caught worshipping an idol, he was to be stoned, without mercy -"Idol worshippers must be stoned"; but if a heathen idol worshipper repented, started seeking the Lord, and wanted to become a proselyte, he was accepted, forgiven, and didn't have to be stoned. If a church council made a decision for church member's conduct, it didn't mean that lost people coming to the church with divorce in their past were treated the same - THE PAST WAS PAST AND FORGIVEN. Even Tertullian, who believed that marrying again after the death of your first mate was sinful and wrong, said the following about Paul's clear instructions in I Cor. 7: **(Tertullian)** *"Thou hast been bound to a wife, seek not loosing; thou hast been loosed from a wife, seek not a wife." "But if thou shalt have*

29

taken to thyself a wife, thou hast not sinned;" **because to one who, before believing, had been** *"loosed from a wife,"* **she will not be counted a** *second* **wife who, subsequently to believing, is the** *first;* **for it is from the time of our believing that our life itself dates its origin."** Tertullian was one of the strictest on monogamy, but here he shares WHY we don't find any divorce before baptism!!! They gave everyone a fresh start at conversion. "LIFE BEGINS AT CONVERSION"

❖ They never demand remarried converts to divorce - there is no evidence of this at all.

❖ They don't know about an espousal theory, but all believe the "exception clause" is speaking of "immorality".

❖ They are usually holding up an ideal (a general rule) against pagan or Jewish licentiousness, and not dealing with exceptions.

❖ Those who deal with divorce and remarriage are usually 100 years or more removed from the apostles.

❖ They are usually tainted with the ascetic trends of the age on this subject especially. Those who were against second marriages are also against widows remarrying. Athenagoras calls the second marriage of a widow or widower a "cloaked adultery". This reveals their departure from the apostles on this subject.

So, we must look to God's Word for the truth. The early church writings show strong departure from simple apostolic faith even in the second and third century concerning baptism, ritualism, asceticism, allegorical speculations, etc.

The earliest I have found this absolute "no divorce, no remarriage" belief as an official church position is in the Roman Catholic Church around the tenth century. Thomas Aquinas and his contemporaries taught this along with the selling of indulgences and the other Romish abominations. During the reformation, the Catholics were the ones who were against divorce and remarriage under any condition. I believe this stemmed from other erroneous ideas about marriage, like: The Holy Ghost left the room when a husband and wife had intercourse, because it was sinful even for them; they couldn't have intercourse on Sunday because it was the day of the resurrection, on Monday in honor of the faithful dead, on Thursday because of Jesus' arrest, on Friday for the Crucifixion, and on Saturday for the virgin Mary; and what they did on the only remaining days (Tuesday and Wednesday) had to be confessed to the priest. This type of teaching led to forced celibacy for the clergy and nuns, which led to gross sin and embarrassing failures.

The Protestants, though holding to a position similar to mine, still didn't let go of all the Catholic error. Martin Luther said that intercourse is never without sin, but God allowed it by his grace.

The true Anabaptists held a sensible, Scriptural view about the marriage relationship. I believe they were correct. The view that I present is essentially the same as the Anabaptists. The Mennonites changed to the "no divorce, no remarriage" position around 1800 it seems. I speculate from what I've read and observed that this took place as follows: They, being ostracized from society by continual persecutions, began to think and teach concerning their *own group* without much interaction with the outside. Indeed it would be wrong for someone in *their group* to divorce their mate and marry another woman in the group. This would not be allowed under any condition. So, they established beliefs dealing with believers in their *own group*. When they then met with someone from the *outside* who was on a second marriage, they had a dilemma: "We can't allow them in, or it will violate what we have been teaching". I believe this is how they changed from their forefathers who were dealing more in evangelism with lost and unlearned people. I believe Satan has used this to strangle their evangelism, which it has very much hindered. Most people who hold this erroneous view do so because they deem it "safer"; but you can't improve on truth. Truth is always the safest position to take. Truth protects the established church AND makes room for converts from the world.

3

In The Beginning

"And the LORD God caused a deep sleep to fall upon Adam, and he slept: and he took one of his ribs, and closed up the flesh instead thereof; and the rib, which the LORD God had taken from man, made he a woman, and brought her unto the man. And Adam said, This is now bone of my bones, and flesh of my flesh: she shall be called Woman, because she was taken out of Man. Therefore shall a man leave his father and his mother, and shall cleave unto his wife: and they shall be one flesh. And they were both naked, the man and his wife, and were not ashamed." Gen. 2:21-24

In order to rightly understand the marriage, divorce, and remarriage issue, we must start at the beginning and fully understand its development. This way we can comprehend the mind frame in which Jesus and the apostles spoke about the subject. If we don't understand the Old Testament, we will never understand the New. Most of the passages in the New Testament dealing with marriage, divorce, and remarriage (which are often wrongly applied), are based on the Law of the Old Testament, and consistent with God's Law. In Romans 7 Paul is speaking to them who "know the Law"; and in I Cor. 7 Paul speaks of being "bound by the Law." John the Baptist tells Herod it is "unlawful" for him to have Herodias. All these and more are based on the Law; so we must understand the Law. All this is also evidence that Jesus didn't do away with what the law said concerning marriage, but only corrected erroneous interpretations of the law.

The New Testament is clear that Christians are to fulfill the "righteousness of the Law". This is done by following the Spirit in obedience to the Law of Christ. The point is that the righteousness of the Old Testament, when properly understood, is not obsolete - but is absolute. God's morality has never changed. Jesus rightly interpreted the Law according to God's original intent. Much can be gleaned from God's original statements about his design for marriage. By walking in the Spirit, we fulfill the righteousness of the Law, because the Holy Spirit is the one who inspired the Law -- It is God's Law!

■ ONLY ONE RIB

God took only one rib, and made only one wife for Adam. Although Polygamy was later tolerated, it was not God's original will for marriage. Moses didn't write the Pentateuch until about 2500 years after Adam and Eve's marriage. There was probably oral law and some writings before Moses wrote the Law, but man's spiritual perception was dim, and God dealt with what little he had to work with in mercy and wisdom.

The Law didn't prohibit polygamy, but, instead, regulated it. God even told David that he had given him his wives; which shows God's toleration of the practice at that time. God allowed polygamy, I believe, out of merciful wisdom. Times were rough; and usually only rich men had more than one wife. These women were taken care of, fed, clothed, protected and better off than if God stopped the practice abruptly, leaving them destitute. God's people were also allowed to multiply quicker under this arrangement. Because polygamy was already very common, God, for that time period, only put restrictions and regulations on it. In the New Testament churches under the apostles it seems clear that they accepted and "grandfathered in" those with more than one wife; but it was frowned upon, and I don't believe a member would be allowed to take a second wife. A Bishop, who was to be the example for the members, had to be the husband of "one wife".

■ ONE FLESH

Based on Adam and Eve's example of marriage, Moses states, "Therefore shall a man leave his father and mother, and shall cleave unto his wife: and they shall be one flesh." God acted as their father, for he actually was. Notice that the "one flesh" idea is in the same sentence with speaking of the transfer of relationship from family to wife. God made and brought Eve to Adam. God intended for the fathers to help find a wife for their sons. God intended for the bride's father to have the authority to approve and give his daughter to the groom. The groom was then to leave the bond of "oneness" that he had with his family, and cleave to his wife. The bride and groom were then to become "one flesh". They both left previous family oneness and became one. God gave them a wedding ceremony, and parental approval.

Marriage is more than a physical union. The physical union is a large part, but the context of the "oneness" is set in contrast to that of the bride and groom with their parents: the oneness of mind, heart, and purpose. Adam and Eve became one in body (naked and unashamed) and one in heart (leaving parents and cleaving to each other). Those who overemphasize this "one flesh" connection in saying it can never be broken have to ignore the fact that God allowed it to be broken in His Law, and Paul equates it with a connection to a harlot, which must be broken. It ought not to be broken in marriage, but it is possible, and sometimes necessary and righteous to break it

■ COVENANT OF COMPANIONSHIP

Marriage is ultimately a covenant of companionship. This companionship is what man needed when God said it was not good for man to be alone. People who have not the gift for singleness should not be looked upon as simply wanting sexual relations, but as needing companionship. We find this concept, of marriage being a covenant of companionship, clearly set forth in Malachi 2:14,

"Yet ye say, Wherefore? Because the LORD hath been witness between thee and the wife of thy

youth, against whom thou hast dealt treacherously: yet is she thy companion, and the wife of thy covenant."

Notice, the idea here of a wife is that, "she is thy companion by covenant". Companionship is the ultimate reason for marriage. This companionship is formed by a covenant. This includes vows one to another. It is a contractual agreement that God also binds in the Heavens, because he is the designer of it.

This covenant of companionship is what makes us eligible for sexual union without sin. Sexual union is not a covenant, nor does it make the covenant; it is simply a benefit that comes with living in a marriage covenant. Only in the context of this covenant is the bed undefiled. Some married couples are incapable of sexual union, but are still companions and married. God said it was not good for man to be alone, and then made a help meet (fitting) for him.

We see in I Cor. 6 that being joined to a harlot produces a "one flesh" union; but only the minimum of physical unity; and not a marriage that God has instituted. Fornication and marriage are not the same. In fornication, though becoming one in body temporarily, there are not two cleaving together to form a family in submission to God's order--no covenant of companionship; no parental consent; no ceremony, etc. Simply shacking up is in rebellion to God's order. Irregular marriage, such as incestuous relations, sodomy, etc. is never acceptable before God. I Cor. 6, however, does show that being "one flesh" is not always a "once for all" and "unbreakable" arrangement as some erroneously teach.

It is very sad that many marriages today, though they include the cleaving in submission to God's order of marriage (as opposed to fornication); yet with selfish unregenerate hearts, they can never become one in heart as God intended. One or both are in it to "get", and not to "give". No marriage can be even close to what God intends until Jesus is Lord in the hearts of both individuals. However, the marriages of the lost are still recognized by God, and they are still accountable to maintain the covenant.

The Scriptural usage of the word "adultery" generally has in view the breaking of this covenant of companionship by the introduction of a third party - the "strange" woman or man. This adulterates the pure mixture of husband and wife in a covenant relationship. Adam and Eve were not threatened with this in any way (at first); and thus had perfect companionship. The introduction of a second wife, however, was not considered adultery or the breaking of the marriage covenant, unless the first wife was thereby neglected – this was looked upon as a breach of the covenant, and the wife was free to divorce her husband and leave in this case (Ex. 21:11). The Levirate marriage was not considered adultery either, because it was according to God's Law. A man could take another wife, but the woman could not take another man while still married. The woman was considered the property of the man, not the other way around.

Though the woman was put under man's authority through sin, yet previous to sin, there was perfect sharing and mutual love. The woman was part of Adam himself, taken from his breast, near his heart;

and there was true oneness. Sin brought pride, and pride produced contention.

Adam did have seniority even before the fall, because she was created to be his helper; and had she recognized this position, she would have asked him before assuming to take the forbidden fruit, which might have saved her from falling. This caused God to decree that from now on her desire was to be to her husband (she must ask him first), and he would rule over her.

■ ONLY BY PRIDE COMETH CONTENTION (Prov. 13:10)

When sin came, there were some provisions that had to be made to deal with sin and its results. Every law is due to the hardness of men's hearts; because the law is for transgressors. It tells what to do when sin happens. I **Tim. 1:9 tells us, "The law is not made for a righteous man, but for the lawless and disobedient, for the ungodly and for sinners...".** Due to sin, the woman was put under the man's authority; there was need for clothing and modesty; and as people multiplied, there had to be laws made dealing with the fruits of sin. Sinful man could not enjoy fully what Adam and Eve had originally had, and provisions had to be made for the hardness of men's sinful hearts. Greed, lust, pride, selfishness, death, etc. took their toll on marriage, and God had to then regulate man's sinful conduct in order to restrain its effects. Unless God eradicated sin, his perfect design for marriage could not be expected of mankind.

Why didn't God have to make laws about marriage for

Adam and Eve? There was no sin. There could be no adultery, lust, hate, selfishness, or death in the Garden of Eden. As soon as man sinned, the marriage ideal failed to be reality with everyone; and laws had to be made so rulers knew what to do when sin happened.

4

Marriage Under Moses

"Marriage is honorable in all, and the bed undefiled: but whoremongers and adulterers God will judge." Heb. 13:4

This chapter should be titled, "Marriage under God" – that is if you believe, "Holy men of old spake as they were moved by the Holy Ghost" (2 Peter 1:21); and "All scripture is given by inspiration of God, and is profitable for doctrine, for reproof, for correction, for instruction in righteousness:" (2 Tim. 3:16). What Scriptures had Timothy known from a child? It is speaking of the Old Testament.

Many wrongly teach that God "winked" (Acts 17:30) at all divorce and remarriage in the Old Testament, but now commands every man to repent of it. However, in Acts 17:30, Paul is speaking about God overlooking man's improper worship and false concepts about the Godhead (vss. 24-29). God didn't overlook all divorce and remarriage as we will see. He doesn't now command everyone to repent of his own

41

law, but of their ignorance -- because he now offers them light and regeneration. This regeneration allows us to fulfill the righteousness of the law (Romans 8); it doesn't cause us to repent of the law. Fulfilling the righteousness of the law means you are living a life against which there is no law (Gal. 5:22, 23). You don't need the laws about adultery, because you are chaste. You don't need laws about divorce, because you and your wife are following Jesus. The problem is that not all people live righteous. If my wife forsakes the faith, commits adultery, etc. what am I to do? This is when we need a law.

■ **Deut. 22:13-21**

"If any man take a wife, and go in unto her, and hate her, and give occasions of speech against her, and bring up an evil name upon her, and say, I took this woman, and when I came to her, I found her not a maid: Then shall the father of the damsel, and her mother, take and bring forth the tokens of the damsel's virginity unto the elders of the city in the gate: And the damsel's father shall say unto the elders, I gave my daughter unto this man to wife, and he hateth her; and, lo he hath given occasions of speech against her, saying, I found not thy daughter a maid; and yet these are the tokens of my daughter's virginity. And they shall spread the cloth before the elders of the city. And the elders of that city shall take that man and chastise him; and they shall amerce him in an hundred shekels of silver, and give them unto the father of the damsel, because he hath brought up an evil name upon a virgin of Israel: and she shall be his wife; he may not put her away all his days. But if this thing be true, and the tokens of

virginity be not found for the damsel: Then they shall bring out the damsel to the door of her father's house, and the men of the city shall stone her with stones that she die: because she hath wrought folly in Israel, to play the whore in her father's house: so shalt thou put away evil from among you."

Sexual sin in an espoused bride, even if detected during the marriage night, was punished with death. This means the man had full right to dissolve the marriage covenant (through death) and marry again because of this sin, even though he had already had intercourse with the woman. It is important to see that the penalty for unfaithfulness during the betrothal period was equal to the penalty for adultery after the consummation of the marriage.

If the man was wrong, and evidently operating by evil motives, he was unable to ever put her away later (for a less than adultery offense -Deut. 24). This is important to remember. Originally divorce was allowed only for "less than adultery" issues. It wasn't used for adultery at the first, because death was always the penalty. This man forfeited this allowance, due to his evil behavior. If this wife later committed adultery, she would be killed, not put away.

Notice this part of the law is regulating the results of sin. Paul tells us the law wasn't made for a righteous man, but for sinners. We can see this here. The law is dealing with what to do when sin happens. Since sin is a reality, God tells us how to deal with it. God's righteous judgments are still the same (Romans 1:32); because sin is still a reality. Before he executes his judgments, he is now calling men to repentance and remission of sin through Christ. The point I want you to see is that those who didn't commit the adultery, but ended the marriage and remarried (due to adultery) were not under the condemnation of the law.

- ■ **Deut. 22:22,**

"If a man be found lying with a woman married to an husband, then they shall both of them die..."

Sexual sin again gave license to dissolve the marriage covenant, and being that this was done (or supposed to be done by death), the offended party was free to start over. If the man that died had been married, his wife also was free to remarry.

- ■ **Deut. 22:23, 24**

"If a damsel that is a virgin be betrothed unto an husband, and a man find her in the city and lie with her; then ye shall bring them both out unto the gate of the city, and ye shall stone them with stones that they die; the damsel, because she cried not, being in the city; and the man, because he hath humbled his neighbor's wife: so shalt thou put away evil from among you."

Again, sexual sin gave license to the offended parties to start over. It was a righteous thing to dissolve the wedding covenants, when immorality was committed. The penalty for this sin during betrothal was the same as for married people. The woman who was betrothed was called the man's wife. Mary and Joseph were also called husband and wife before they came together in marital intimacy. The covenant was intact during the Jewish betrothal and was just as binding before sexual union as it was after.

■ **Deut. 22:25-29,**

"But if a man find a betrothed damsel in the field, and the man force her, and lie with her: then the man only that lay with her shall die: But unto the damsel thou shalt do nothing...For he found her in the field, and the betrothed damsel cried, and there was none to save her."

"If a man find a damsel that is a virgin, which is not betrothed, and lay hold on her, and lie with her, and they be found; Then the man that lay with her shall give unto the damsel's father fifty shekels of silver, and she shall be his wife; because he hath humbled her, he may not put her away all his days."

Because the man's character again was put in question, he could not later put away his wife for less than sexual sin under the Deut. 24 provision. He, like the other man we mentioned earlier, had forfeited the permission to divorce for less than adultery. If this woman later committed adultery, she would be stoned; he would not have to keep her.

It wasn't necessary for the father to consent to giving his daughter to this man, whom she had fornicated with. He could refuse, and just accept a payment for the offense (Ex. 22:16, 17).

■ Numbers 5:12-28,

"Speak unto the children of Israel, and say unto them, If any man's wife go aside, and commit a trespass against him, and a man lie with her carnally, and it be hid from the eyes of her husband, and be kept close, and she be defiled, and there be no witness against her, neither she be taken with the manner; and the spirit of jealousy come upon him, and he be jealous of his wife, and she be defiled: or if the spirit of jealousy come upon him, and he be jealous of his wife, and she be not defiled: Then shall the man bring his wife unto the priest, and he shall bring her offering for her, the tenth part of an ephah of barley meal; he shall pour no oil upon it, nor put frankincense thereon; for it is an offering of jealousy, an offering of memorial, bringing iniquity to remembrance. And the priest shall bring her near, and set her before the LORD: And the priest shall take holy water in an earthen vessel; and of the dust that is in the floor of the tabernacle the priest shall take, and put it into the water: And the priest shall set the woman before the LORD, and uncover the woman's head, and put the offering of memorial in her hands, which is the jealousy offering: and the priest shall have in his hand the bitter water that causeth the curse: And the priest shall charge her by an oath, and say unto the woman, If no man have lain with thee, and if thou hast not gone aside to uncleanness with another instead of thy husband, be thou free from this bitter water that causeth the curse: but if thou hast gone aside to another instead of thy husband, and if thou be defiled, and some man have lain with thee beside thine husband: Then the priest shall charge the woman with an oath of cursing, and the priest shall say unto the woman, The LORD make thee a curse and an oath among thy people, when the LORD doth make thy thigh to rot, and thy belly to swell; And this water that causeth the curse shall go into thy bowels, to make thy belly to swell, and thy thigh to rot: and the woman shall say, Amen, amen. And the priest shall write these curses in a book, and he shall blot them out with the bitter water: And he shall cause the woman to drink the bitter water that causeth the curse: and the water that causeth the curse shall enter into her, and become bitter. Then the priest shall take the jealousy offering out of the woman's hand, and shall wave the offering before the LORD, and offer it upon the altar: And the priest shall take an handful of the offering, even the memorial thereof, and burn it upon the altar, and afterward shall cause the woman to drink the water. And when he hath made her to drink the water, then it shall come to pass, that, if she be defiled, and have done trespass against her husband, that the water that causeth the curse shall enter into her, and become bitter, and her belly shall swell, and her thigh shall rot: and the woman shall be a curse among her people. And if the woman be not defiled, but be clean; then she shall be free, and shall conceive seed. This is the law of jealousies, when a wife goeth aside to another instead of her husband, and is defiled;"

Notice that the husband was fully backed by God to get rid of an adulterous wife. Even if he was suspicious, he could find out. Marriage is God's institution. He alone reserves the right to regulate marriage. Sexual relations are pure and right within God's Law, but are wicked and sinful outside God's

Law. Using God given desires and blessings in a God forbidden way is sinful; while using those same blessings and desires within God's will is righteous. Even polygamy, when allowed by God and used within his regulations wasn't sinful. God sees not as man sees, and knows what is best for his universe.

Due to sin, God had to make laws regulating marriage. Remember that the flood came partly due to sinful marriage practices. Sodom and Gomorrah perished for perverting what God had made pure. What God had given to be one of man's greatest physical blessings has turned to man's greatest snare because of man's sinful desires. The complications that sin brought needed God's answers.

We must keep in mind that all scripture is given by inspiration of God. Moses' Law included the first five books of the Bible, and was God's Word on what he allowed and didn't allow in the institution of marriage. It wasn't necessarily always God's perfect will, but what he allowed, due to man's fallen state.

Due to death, God gave laws concerning the widow. If she had no children, her brother in law was to raise up seed for his deceased brother. This relation may have only lasted as long as it took for her to have a child. This was not considered adultery or fornication, as it was according to God's regulation. This law only had relevance for the Jewish nation to preserve their inheritance in the land. For a man to marry his close relative for any other reason was incest and unlawful. John the Baptist, who lived under the Law, reprimanded Herod for marrying his sister in law; which was also considered incest. His rebuke of

Herod has nothing to do with the divorce and remarriage issue today (as our friends who disagree like to use it). Had Herodias not been Herod's sister in law, it wouldn't have been unlawful, unless she was undivorced.

A wife was bound by the Law to her husband as long as he lived and didn't divorce her (I Cor. 7:39). If she ran off and married another without being lawfully divorced by her husband, she would be guilty of adultery (Rom. 7:1). If the husband died or divorced her, she was then free to marry another without sin.

When two single people were caught in fornication (sexual union outside God's Law); they were to get married (sexual union inside God's Law). If someone was caught in fornication of other sorts, such as homosexuality, whoredom, bestiality, etc. they were to be stoned, burnt, or whatever God had required (Lev. 20).

■ DIVORCE

Moses was obviously confronted with a situation where there was some "uncleanness" found in a wife which was not actual adultery. God inspired him to write the following precept in order to rightly deal with this situation. If we give God's Word and God's man, Moses, due respect, then we will not look upon this as a mistake or embarrassment to God; but the best thing to be done in this situation. God suffered men to divorce a wife due to some "uncleanness" (matter of nakedness), so there could be peace in the home and the wife wouldn't be abused, or her bad example tolerated. She was allowed to remarry, so she could be provided for and protected. This was no mistake, but God's will under the circumstances. We find also that if a man took a second wife, he was not to diminish the provisions of the first wife. If he did, she was free to divorce him (Ex. 21:10, 11). Other matters of divorce were usually stated as the man's move, but women obviously also had legal grounds for divorce at times. If she appealed to the authorities, there were laws that protected her.

■ **Deut. 24:1-4,**

"When a man hath taken a wife, and married her, and it come to pass that she find no favour in his eyes, because he hath found some uncleanness in her: then let him write her a bill of divorcement, and give it in her hand, and send her out of his house. And when she is departed out of his house, she may go and be another man's wife. And if the latter husband hate her, and write her a bill of divorcement, and giveth it in her hand, and sendeth her out of his house; or if the latter husband die, which took her to be his wife; Her former husband, which sent her away, may not take her again to be his wife, after that she is defiled; for that is abomination before the LORD: and thou shalt not cause the land to sin, which the LORD thy God giveth thee for an inheritance."

There are two views of this passage that we should be aware of:

1. Moses, by God's leading, allowed divorce for something other than adultery under these conditions: 1. The bill of divorce, and 2. The former husband not being able to take back a woman who had remarried.

2. The people were already in this practice (probably from Egypt), and this passage is only recognizing divorce; and simply telling the husband, who put away his wife, he could not take her back again once she remarried. Many commentaries agree that the passage should be read as one complete sentence by being translated with the first three verses for the protasis (the supposition clause, which starts with "if"); and verse 4 as the apodosis (the conclusion). It would read like this:

· *"If a man hath taken a wife, and married her, and it come to pass that she doth not find favour in his eye, because of some uncleanness in her, and he hath written her a bill of divorcement, and given it in her hand, and sent her out of his house; and if she hath departed out of his house, and hath gone and become another man's; and if the latter husband hate her, and write her a bill of divorcement, and give it in her hand, and send her out of his house; or if the latter husband who took her to be his wife, die: her former husband, who sent her away, may not take her again to be his wife." (The Pulpit Commentary)*

This would mean that Moses is only recognizing divorce as a legal reality, and forbidding the remarriage to the first husband. **From what Jesus says in speaking with the Pharisees (Mark 10:3-5), it**

seems clear that the first view of this passage is the correct one.

Many wish to choose the second out of embarrassment that Moses allowed divorce – But why? God knows what is best, and this is God's inspired Word. Moses did not make a mistake. To deny the first as being correct means that Moses never taught them to give a writing of divorcement, which in fact he did – according to Jesus and the Jews.

Regardless of which view of Deut. 24 is correct; the following basic facts about the situation are still the same:

1. The word "uncleanness" is the Hebrew term `Ervah (#6172 – Strong's); and literally means, "a matter of nakedness", or "something shameful or repulsive". `Ervah is translated 51 times as "nakedness" in the Old Testament, one time as "shame", and once as "uncleanness". It is commonly assumed that this meant something other than adultery in the light of chapter 22 and other passages where adultery brought death to the offender. It is clear that divorce was known when chapter 22 was written, because the man who falsely accused his new wife, was forbidden to put her away later under this provision. It obviously didn't mean his wife could later commit adultery without penalty. This also shows that "putting away" was originally meant to be for other things than full fledged adultery, which brought death. However, it seems that it did refer to something disgraceful or immoral enough to give sufficient reason to put her away. The sincere man

who made use of this provision surely felt she was unfaithful or had made a breach in the covenant. A sincere man would not use this provision unless he felt it was a righteous thing, and that she deserved it. God obviously only meant this to be used by sincere people, not abused by lustful and selfish men seeking another wife without supporting the first one – as he would have to do in polygamy.

What if an upright Jewish man married a woman and she, in time, began to get drunk while he was gone, and was found to be doing the Bathsheba trick of bathing where men could see her. She began to display herself in public immodestly, was flirtatious or maybe had a foul mouth, etc. No, it was not full fledged adultery, as there was no other individual whom she had relationship with, but she was an adulteress at heart with whomever she was around – this would certainly merit a bill of divorce as a matter of lewdness and "nakedness"; but not qualify for adultery. Another man with less scruple might take her right in.

2. This bill of divorcement dissolved the marriage covenant, and allowed both parties to remarry. For a man to put away his wife simply because he was upset with her, and then marry another seems to be adultery through legal channels. I believe this is what Jesus was saying to the men who thought they were righteous in doing this. This was a civil enactment so the judges would know who to stone, and who not to stone for adultery – It kept false accusations from harming innocent people. This provision was to limit abuse and bring peace among hard hearted people – this was not God's first will for marriage, or the

53

righteous path the Law prescribed for mankind; but was a necessary provision for when sin happened.

3. The divorce and second marriage, though possibly contracted with sinful motivations, was still binding by the law, and still required a bill of divorce, adultery or death to break it. The contracting of the second marriage broke the first marriage obligations. It was a species of adultery to divorce and remarry for something less than what God had in mind when giving this precept, but the second marriage wasn't "continuous adultery" that must be split up by the judges, if they suspected such.

4. Once the remarriage took place, the first marriage was over forever and could not be reconciled at all. It was an abomination to do so. This means it would be worse than even the divorce and remarriage was. The woman was defiled as far as her relationship with the first man was concerned. The second marriage, even if a sinful transaction by a wicked husband, was still binding, and it would be another sin to get another unrighteous divorce. If the woman remarried after the death of the first husband, there is no reason to call her defiled; so the defilement is only in regards to her first husband, and that is why the first husband cannot take her back.

5. The first husband ceased to be her husband, and became her former husband. They ceased to be "one flesh" and became "one flesh" with the person they married. They were not still married to the first "in God's eyes".

If you teach that divorced people are still married in

"God's eyes", then you are saying divorced people can enjoy sexual relations without getting remarried. This is dangerous teaching, and can only lead to fornication. God does not see divorced people as still married.

Moses was trying to keep this practice from being too hasty or common by these regulations. Later in the time of Christ, the Jews were abusing this passage as though it made divorce a righteous act, even for "every cause". They used the passage in Deut. 24 to justify divorcing their wives for "every cause" (Matt 19). There arose much disputation over what "some uncleanness" actually was – a dispute which Jesus authoritatively answered.

In the days of Christ, there were two schools of thought on this issue. The school of Shammai said divorce was only lawful for fornication (immorality), and the school of Hillel said this passage made all divorce for "every cause" lawful. When insincere people seek loopholes instead of righteousness, it is common to see righteous precepts abused for ungodly purposes.

It is clear that God hated unrighteous divorce, even in the Old Testament. In Malachi 2:16 God says he "hateth putting away". Verse 15 tells us that God is seeking a godly seed, which divorce destroys. It is terrible to see the destruction of children due to parent's wicked selfishness in divorce and remarriage. What God allowed to maintain the purity and harmony of marriage, man abused and used to deal treacherously with the bride of his youth.

■ DIVORCE FOR ADULTERY

It is impossible to say exactly when divorce was first allowed to be used instead of stoning for adultery. It may have been started by merciful husbands who would put away their wife under the provision of Deut. 24 instead of making it known they had committed adultery, which would demand death. This seems to be the case with Joseph in Matthew 1:19. In the matter of divorce for adultery, God doesn't condemn the offended party, but his anger about the divorce is directed at the offending party. It is possible that Deut. 24 was originally an option for merciful husbands or hard to determine cases.

No matter when it started, the fact is that it did start. We will see that God approved and even used it himself in dealing with Israel.

"And I saw, when for all the causes whereby backsliding Israel committed adultery I had put her away, and given her a bill of divorce; yet her treacherous sister Judah feared not, but went and played the harlot also." Jer. 3:8

If a married or betrothed person was caught in adultery, originally they were to be stoned. divorce seems to have been substituted for stoning some time early in Israel's history long before the story of Mary and Joseph; because we see God's example of divorcing Israel for spiritual adultery (Jer. 3:8). God obviously accepted this as a substitute for stoning. If Joseph had been innovating contrary to God's Law, he wouldn't have been called "Just" for doing so. We will see that Jesus puts the final stamp of approval on divorce for sexual sin, rather than stoning.

Most likely stoning was later allowed as the highest penalty; but if the offended person had mercy, they could just divorce the offender instead.

It was a "given" that adultery gave license to the offended party to break the marriage covenant (whether by stoning or divorce). This fact is never disputed in the Bible. If the husband didn't demand stoning of his unfaithful wife, evidence shows that divorce was allowed. If the woman in Deut. 24 had been put away for adultery, Moses wouldn't be concerned about her being put away properly, her right to remarriage, or her being defiled by the second marriage. She would have already been defiled by her sin, and at that time, been stoned.

It is a fact that we must deal with, that divorce is a biblical concept allowed and even used by God when sexual sin has marred the marriage covenant. All divorce is caused by sin; but all divorce is not sinful. Without sin, there would be no divorce; but because sin is a reality, divorce is sometimes a necessity. God hates divorce, because God hates what causes divorce; but God didn't sin when he divorced Israel. In the case of Mary and Joseph, the Bible says, ***"Then Joseph her husband, <u>being a just man</u>, and not willing to make her a publick example, was minded to put her away (divorce) privily." (Matt. 1:19).***

Sexual sin, when repented of, didn't require divorce, but allowed divorce. However, if the sexual sin was continued without repentance, divorce was a righteous alternative to living with a harlot. If mercy is showed to the offender, and they are not put to death; this doesn't keep the offended party from being free to remarry. They are not under obligation by the law to reconcile, because the adultery broke that obligation to the marriage covenant. The charge of adultery was always placed on the head of the one who broke the marriage, whether by sexual sin or unrighteous divorce and remarriage. This is made clear by Christ, as we will see. It is sinful to put away your mate because you want someone else. It is sinful to put away your mate because you are tired of their manners; but it is righteous to put away your mate because they persist in sexual sin.

In the Bible, when divorce is allowed, the right to remarry is assumed. The Pharisees knew this, for when they questioned Christ they only asked if divorce was lawful. They didn't ask if remarriage was lawful, because they knew that when divorce is lawful, so is remarriage for the innocent party -- just as it would have been had the offender been stoned instead of divorced.

■ THE WOMAN OF SAMARIA

The "woman at the well", whom Jesus spoke with, had been married and divorced five times; and was now living unmarried with a man. How was the last situation different? It was not a marriage! Jesus himself said, "Thou hast had five husbands, and he whom thou now hast is not thy husband". The first five were law-binding marriages, where the sexual relation was lawful; but the last was sexual sin, and not binding by the law. The last situation would not have required a bill of divorce, but the others did. The last situation would have produced bastard children, but not the former.

Most likely this woman was put away by wicked selfish men five different times. After being so degraded and defiled, she simply lived with the last unmarried. Chances are, she had never been unfaithful to any of her husbands, but was put away unrighteously: her husbands using Deut. 24 as their excuse. No doubt, she would probably have carried a stigma after five marriages, but the marriages were still marriages, not just fornication, like the last one. This situation illustrates the abuse of Deut. 24 at the time of Christ.

■ GOD AND ISRAEL

God divorced Israel, and then asked her to come back. This was lawful because in this scenario, she had not married again. This should have really spoken to Israelite men and women -- The men would have never taken some unfaithful woman back, when they could start with a fresh one; and the women knew they would never be wanted back, if they were unfaithful.

God's example through Hosea is also a powerful message to Israel in this very way. It was unheard of! God set the mind-boggling example of forgiveness and reconciliation, even to an adulteress wife! God has set this example for us: 1. The act of lawful divorce, and 2. When there is repentance before remarriage to another; forgiveness and reconciliation of the first marriage. **Notice, though, that God wasn't required to take Israel back, and couldn't if she didn't repent.**

■ EZRA AND NEHEMIAH

Many use the situation in Ezra and Nehemiah to teach that we must separate remarried persons, but this passage is not in their favor. In Ezra and Nehemiah Israelites had married unbelievers (Gentiles). This intermingling with unbelievers was a great cause for apostasy, and therefore was forbidden, except on certain occasions (Deut. 21:10-13 compare with Deut. 7:3, and Josh. 23:12,13).

These people were intermarrying with foreigners who were not proselytes. Ezra and Nehemiah made them put away these foreign wives. As we know (and will speak more of later), in the New Testament, if a person is married to an unbeliever, they are NOT to divorce on this account, but try to win them. So, where, in the Old Testament, we have a command to separate, we have a command to stay together in the New Testament for the sake of the children and winning the lost mate (I Cor. 7). This is important to remember as we continue our study. In the New Testament, as in the Old Testament, believers are not supposed to marry unbelievers. If this happens, though, there is not forced divorce; but repentance on the part of the believer – who must now be faithful first to Christ, even if they lose the unbeliever – see I Cor. 7

It is important to notice that all the laws and regulations we have just covered were for God's covenant people; not Gentile, uncircumcised, unbelievers. Surely, the unbeliever's hearts were harder, and more ignorant than God's chosen people.

REVIEW

1. Because the reality of sin in fallen man affected marriage, God's ideal was no longer fully possible.
2. God set down laws showing what we can righteously do when sin happens.
3. For adultery, it was always righteous to dissolve the marriage covenant, whether by stoning or divorce.
4. Righteous divorce gave permission for righteous remarriage.
5. Divorce for the "matter of nakedness" with the bill of divorce left the parties free to remarry.
6. Unrighteous divorce (abuse of Deut. 24) would leave people obligated to repent and reconcile.
7. Whether according to Moses' intentions, or in abuse of them, remarriage after divorce, as instituted in Deut. 24, was still a binding marriage, and could only be broken by another divorce or death.
8. Once the remarriage took place, the first marriage could never be righteously renewed – This was strictly forbidden. God could have strictly forbidden all divorce, but chose not to.
9. According to God's Law, anything that had the penalty of death (like apostasy) would also free the innocent person to remarry, due to the death of the mate. We also saw that a woman could leave if the husband, in taking another wife, diminished her provisions – i.e. did not uphold his end of the marriage covenant.

5

What Did Jesus Teach?

As we come to the New Testament with a better understanding of the God's Law, I believe it will be easier to understand what Jesus is teaching, and why some were surprised. Due to having double motives, the people had not recognized the true intent of the law, but were caught up in misconceptions.   It is common for sinful men to look for loopholes to fulfill their sinful desires without appearing as wicked as they are. The religious leaders of Jesus' day were divided on this issue of divorce. The Jews, for the most part, were very loose in using what they considered their loophole -- Deut. 24. They interpreted Deut. 24 to mean they could divorce their wife for "every cause", as long as they gave her a proper bill of divorce. They were cloaked adulterers through legal channels. They were resting in their abuse of the "letter" of the Law, instead of striving to obey the "spirit" of the Law.

A close and thorough study of the New Testament will reveal that Jesus is not teaching contrary to God's Law, but just interpreting it in its true spirit and light, while refuting false concepts that had been established. This is very important, as there are those who teach that Jesus' Kingdom Laws showed Moses' Law to be in error. This false teaching was one of the major tenets of Gnosticism. The Gnostics believed that the Old Testament God and Creator of the material universe was a bad God, and not the same as the Father of Jesus Christ. They took this position because they misunderstood Jesus as teaching contrary to the Old Testament. They assumed the bad God taught you could divorce, but the good God taught that you couldn't. The bad God commanded killing and judgment, but the good God taught love, grace and pacifism; etc.

The Gnostics were heretics, and so is everyone who assumes that Jesus is teaching contrary to His own inspired Word. They obviously forget that Jesus was the Logos (Word) of God made flesh, and that it was Jesus who inspired Moses to write what He wrote. They forget that Moses' Law (God's Law) was the church standard for the first twelve years after Pentecost for everyone, and the moral Law was to be written on the hearts of men as the basis for the New Covenant, etc. etc. "Moses Law" was the Scripture Paul was speaking of when he said in **2Tim. 3:16 All scripture is given by inspiration of God, and is profitable for doctrine, for reproof, for correction, for instruction in righteousness: 17 That the man of God may be perfect, throughly furnished unto all good works.**

Jesus came to vindicate the Spirit and Righteousness of the Law, and correct misconceptions; but not to correct His own Law:

■ **Matt. 5:17-20,**

"Think not that I am come to destroy the law, or the prophets: I am not come to destroy, but to fulfil[*]. For verily I say unto you, Till heaven and earth pass, one jot or one tittle shall in no wise pass from the law, till all be fulfilled. Whosoever therefore shall break one of these least commandments, and shall teach men so, he shall be called the least in the <u>kingdom of heaven</u>: but whosoever shall do and teach them, the same shall be called great in the <u>kingdom of heaven</u>. For I say unto you, that except your righteousness shall exceed the righteousness of the scribes and pharisees, ye shall in no case enter into the <u>kingdom of heaven</u>."

The part of the law that was done away in Christ was the part fulfilled, which included all the types and shadows. The moral aspects of the law were carried over and included in the Law of Christ – and written on our hearts as the basis of the New Covenant. The Pharisees and Scribes only practiced outward conformity to accepted standards established by their peers and common interpretations of the day. They generally did not have a "heart holiness" that sought God's will, but did what could be seen of men (for personal advantage), and no more (Matt. 23). Unless

---

[*] This is the same Greek word used in Romans 8:4, "That the righteousness of the law might be <u>fulfilled</u> in us, who walk not after the flesh, but after the Spirit."

you have a heart to seek and do God's will, rather than look for loopholes, you will not make it into Christ's Kingdom! Your righteousness must exceed the righteousness of the Scribes and Pharisees. You must strive to obey the "spirit" or "intent" of God's moral Law, not just have outward conformity to the "letter" of the Law.

■ **Matt. 5:21-22,**

"Ye have heard that it was said by them of old time, Thou shalt not kill; and whosoever shall kill shall be in danger of the judgment: but I say unto you, That whosoever is angry with his brother without a cause shall be in danger of the judgment: and whosoever shall say to his brother, Raca, shall be in danger of the council: but whosoever shall say, Thou fool, shall be in danger of hell fire."

Notice he says, and will say many times, "Ye have heard that it was said..."; and not, "It is written", as he did when speaking to Satan (Matt. 4). Jesus is dealing with misconceptions. They thought that since the law said, Thou shalt not kill; they could do everything but kill. This concept was because they were not looking for God's will, but looking to justify their wrong. Listen to Leviticus 19:18, "Thou shalt not avenge, nor bear any grudge against the children of thy people, but thou shalt love thy neighbour as thyself: I am the LORD." Isn't this interesting! If you read the rest of what Jesus said in vss. 23-26 on this subject, you will find him simply teaching and applying the Old Testament Law of Moses in its proper light.

■ **Matt. 5:27-28,**

"Ye have heard that it was said by them of old time, Thou shalt not commit adultery: but I say unto you, That whosoever looketh on a woman to lust after her hath committed adultery with her already in his heart."

The scribes had only emphasized one aspect of committing adultery, but they forgot about, "Thou shalt not covet thy neighbor's wife." Jesus is teaching heart holiness, which is the "spirit" or "righteousness" of the law. He is not making void the law, but establishing the law (Romans 3:31). Notice the vigilance he wants us to have against sin. He speaks of plucking out the eye, and cutting off the foot, etc. Now, all agree this is not to be taken literal; but we are to amputate from our life that which causes us to sin against God. Our eyes and hands are passive, not active in sin. They are not to blame. Our heart is the problem. If our heart is seeking God, we will avoid sin with the same vigilance as that of plucking out the eye. NOTE: Just as Jesus calls the wanton look adultery, so next he shows that divorce and remarriage without sufficient cause is technically adultery also. For a man to put away his wife with a bill of divorce; but not with sincere desire to please God; and not for a sufficient "matter of nakedness", as Moses' had in mind, is simply adultery through legal channels.

■ **Matt. 5:31-32,**

"It hath been said, Whosoever shall put away his wife, let him give her a writing of divorcement: but I

say unto you, That whosoever shall put away his wife, saving for the cause of fornication, causeth her to commit adultery: and whosoever shall marry her that is divorced committeth adultery."

This reveals the loose attitude toward divorce among the Jews. "If you want to get rid of your wife, just give her a bill of divorce" -- no big deal. Jesus teaches that to divorce your spouse when they have not violated wedlock through immorality technically causes the resulting remarriage to be adulterous. To marry a woman who is not free from her first marriage obligation is adulterous-Why? The divorce was an abuse of the Law, and therefore you have not gained true freedom in the eyes of the Lawgiver – God Almighty. She and her husband should be repenting and reconciling, and you are keeping her from reconciliation; therefore, you are helping to break the marriage. If the divorce is due to fornication, then the remarriage is not adulterous, because the fornication truly broke the marriage and the obligation to reconcile.

It seems Jesus must be defining the "matter of nakedness" that God said was required to allow the bill of divorce with the word "fornication". He is settling the controversy with an authoritative answer, and giving the proper interpretation of God's Law on the subject. He doesn't say, "except for adultery"; but "except for fornication" – porneia: which includes immorality of many sorts: Moral perversion, incest, homosexuality, prostitution, adultery, bestiality, etc. He seems to say that the only "matter of nakedness" that God accepts as a sufficient ground for divorce is moral or sexual impurity which would fall under the classification of fornication and therefore be a breach of the marriage covenant. God definitely would not accept "every cause" like the Jews settled for as their interpretation of the "matter of nakedness". Thus Jesus is giving the original intent of God's Law, and vindicating Moses. **In our day we use the same Greek word to speak of matters of nakedness when we speak of "pornography" – from the Greek "porneia".**

Being that Shammai and Hillel argued this very point that Jesus is addressing; and being that Rabbi Shammai interpreted Moses' "matter of nakedness" by the word "fornication"; isn't it natural to see that Jesus' use of "fornication" in the same controversy with the same people is for the same purpose? What else would Jesus be doing, but giving the proper interpretation of the Word of God?

What if a godly man with a good testimony had worked hard to raise godly children; but as time went on his wife began showing signs of moral perversion. She began taking drugs, going around the house blatantly immodest, using foul language, viewing pornography (TV, internet, magazines), dressing in skimpy clothes and showing herself in public, getting her hair spiked, piling on the makeup, -- maybe she got a tattoo or did some body piercing, etc. etc. Now, none of this can be classified as "adultery"; and there may be no other individual man that she is involved with; but it can be classified as immorality or "porneia", as she has become a harlot at heart, and has, in a sense, been prostituting herself with society in general. A godly husband should put this woman out of his house, and away from his children. If a woman began going to the bar, dressing immodest and dancing with other men, she could not be charged with adultery; but she is definitely guilty of immorality and is violating the marriage covenant. If a woman rebelled against her husband, and got a job as a waitress at a topless bar, she could not, in this, be charged with adultery; but she is definitely violating the marriage covenant through immorality – a "matter of nakedness" and moral lewdness.

In His statement, Jesus sanctions the practice of divorce for immorality, rather than just stoning; and also sets divorce for other reasons in its proper light. Those wanting to just get another wife used Deut. 24 as a loophole; focusing only on the "permission" Moses granted, not on God's attitude toward the deed. Jesus said that unrighteous divorce left the two obligated to reconcile, and while they were under obligation to reconcile, remarriage for either was adulterous. According to Jesus, Deut. 24 was only to be used for matters serious enough to fall under "fornication" or "whoredom".   This could include a number of things other than adultery.   The Hebrew allowed the divorce for a "matter of nakedness" as we saw earlier -- Jesus uses the word "porneia", which includes a wide range of impurity of many sorts. Jesus' primary point to the Jews was that for someone to divorce their spouse for the express reason of marrying another, and not due to sufficient evil in the spouse was adulterous, and a misuse of God's Law.

"Whoever puts away his wife so he can get another is committing adultery through legal channels, and whoever marries the woman thus put away is engaging in the adultery."

69

Rather than going on through the Sermon on the Mount to show further that Jesus is not changing, but properly applying the law (see our sermon series "The Sermon On The Mount"); we will proceed to His other teaching on marriage. In Matthew 19 some Pharisees come to test Jesus with a question concerning a controversy about Deut. 24.

■ **Matt. 19:3,**

"The Pharisees also came unto him, tempting him, and saying unto him, Is it lawful for a man to put away his wife for every cause?"

Notice they didn't ask if "divorce" was lawful, but if "divorce for every cause" was lawful. Jesus proceeds to tell them that their faulty ideas were due to ignoring God's full counsel in the Law; and His intentions for the Law.   He also tells them what **"cause"** was lawful.

The Pharisees, who were only concerned with outward conformity and doing as they pleased, had focused on Duet.   24 as making divorce and remarriage for "every cause" "lawful." They actually allowed men to put away their wives for burning their food; a bad temper; or because they saw someone they liked better. We have already spoken about the two schools of Shammai and Hillel, who argued this point. Jesus shows the Pharisees their fault by taking them to Genesis to show them what God intended-- His original intent.   <u>Many miss the point that Genesis is also part of the Law of Moses -- but not the part they were looking at.</u>   One who really wants to know God's will looks at the whole counsel of God, not just their supposed "proof text" or "loophole".

When Jesus asked them what Moses commanded, they went directly to Deut. 24 instead of Genesis -- this showed their root problem. They took one passage by itself without the tempering aspect of the other. This is where most people err today also. Upon this basis, Jesus reveals the reason why Moses tolerated divorce: because the people were sinful and hardhearted in their fallen state. The Jew's pride was greatly deflated by the fact that their justification for their divorces was based on a part of the Law which was given, not as a righteous standard, but as a restraint and regulation for fallen sinful man.   The Law was given because mankind was now a fallen race, and the Law told leaders what to do when sin happened -- how to righteously deal with sin and fallen society.

Based on the Pharisees' line of reasoning, polygamy and concubinage would also be righteous; but just because the law didn't directly forbid something, didn't make it God's first will or a righteous standard. Jesus makes it clear that those who will make it into Christ's Kingdom will not be asking, "What can I get by with?" but "What pleases God?" This caused monogamy to be restored as the rule for Christians in the New Testament.

■   **Matt. 19:4-6,**

"And he answered and said unto them, Have ye not read, that he which made them at the beginning made them male and female, and said, For this cause shall a man leave father and mother, and shall cleave

to his wife: and they twain shall be one flesh? Wherefore they are no more twain, but one flesh. What therefore God hath joined together, let not man put asunder."

Here Jesus takes them to the part of the Law they were ignoring. ALL HERESY COMES FROM SEARCHING SCRIPTURE WITH PARTIALITY.

Genesis shows God's original intent; but Deuteronomy tells us what righteous steps to take when sin happens.   A sincere man who understood God's original intent might still have to make use of Deut. 24 in order to maintain purity in his own life – if his wife was caught in immorality of some sort – or a past secret was discovered.   It would be faulty to assume that everyone who made use of Deut. 24 was doing so for sinful reasons. Some have erroneously stated that Jesus took us back to the "Law of Eden" because he quoted Genesis. Jesus is showing them the "original intent"; but is not re-establishing the "Law of Eden". What God spoke in Eden had never been "un-established"; but now that man had fallen, sin had to be dealt with. Jesus goes on to speak of "fornication", "divorce", and "remarriage" none of which were in the "Law of Eden". After quoting Genesis he says, "And I say unto you...", then deals with things not covered in Genesis.   Jesus understood that the Law was a necessary and righteous format for dealing with fallen man - a dynamic that didn't exist in Eden.

I have heard some declare, "What therefore God hath joined together, no man can put asunder!" But this is simply not true. This is like saying, "no man can sin"; just because God said not to. Jesus, in saying, "let not man put asunder", was saying two things: 1. Let not man commit immorality, and thus cause the need for divorce; and 2. Let not any man divorce for something less than immorality. Do not put asunder until God says you should put asunder! God ordained HOW to put asunder by stoning or divorce, which he used himself, when sin broke the marriage covenant.

Jesus has made a New Covenant with man. If we are faithful to believe and follow, we will be saved; but if we rebel and turn away from Christ; he is not obligated or bound to keep his end of the covenant! He is not bound to keep me if I violate the covenant. In salvation God has joined together and basically says, "Let not man put asunder"; but it is still possible for me to rebel and put asunder what God has joined. How surprising that so many who are against the "Eternal Security" teaching in salvation - because "if we break the covenant, God is not bound to keep us" - turn around and teach the opposite of the covenant of marriage - i.e. that both are bound to the covenant for life, even though one breaks the covenant.

Divorce is not God's will, just as immorality is not God's will -- but when sin happens, divorce is sometimes a necessity - a God ordained step. Remember the example God set for us with Israel, in seeking after the offender? Jesus didn't make this example into law, but it is God's perfect will for us to seek to win the sinner. God divorced Israel for continued immorality. He tried to win her back; but couldn't take her back until she repented. Jesus didn't require the offended party to woo the offender. That would be a very high degree of mercy and love, which wasn't demanded, but exemplified. Jesus and Moses

(God's inspired lawgiver) agree fully that divorce and remarriage are allowed for immorality - which includes more than just adultery; but also "matters of nakedness" or lewdness and perversion.

■ **Matt. 19:7-9,**

"They say unto him, Why did Moses then command to give a writing of divorcement, and to put her away? He saith unto them, Moses because of the hardness of your hearts suffered you to put away your wives: but from the beginning it was not so. And I say unto you, Whosoever shall put away his wife, except it be for fornication, and shall marry another, committeth adultery: and whoso marrieth her which is put away doth commit adultery. His disciples say unto him, If the case of the man be so with his wife, it is not good to marry. But he said unto them, All men cannot receive this saying, save they to whom it is given....He that is able to receive it, let him receive it."

The taking of a second wife (polygamy) was never called adultery in the Old Testament. However to take a second wife to the neglect of the first was considered cause for divorce, and therefore a breach of the marriage covenant. Adultery is a crime against your mate in violating the marriage covenant – polygamy in itself did not do this. Therefore Jesus is speaking of adultery as what this whole transaction is technically producing since there is violation of the marriage covenant contrary to God's Law. Jesus is telling us what happens when Deut. 24 is used to justify divorce for reasons other that what God intended – to get another wife or to get out from under covenant responsibilities. In Mark 10 we see that this adultery was a crime against the first mate in breaking wedlock without them being guilty of violating the covenant of marriage first through immorality. To use God's Law to cover a course which is motivated by a wicked heart does not make the transaction righteous before God, even if it appears so before men.

■ Important points concerning what Jesus said:

1. Notice the difference between the Pharisees' viewpoint, "Moses commanded", and Jesus' "Moses suffered" – God's wisdom chose to allow divorce under certain circumstances due to the hardness of fallen men's hearts.

2. Jesus establishes again the lawfulness of divorce for immorality. This exception clause obviously refers to both the divorce and remarriage; otherwise Jesus is not making sense. There is no way to separate the exception from the whole thrust of the sentence. Divorce and remarriage, except for the cause of fornication, is adultery. To state that, WHOSOEVER SHALL PUT AWAY HIS WIFE, EVEN IF FOR FORNICATION, AND SHALL MARRY ANOTHER, COMMITTETH ADULTERY is to state the exact OPPOSITE of what Jesus said; but many teach this as the interpretation of Jesus' words!

3. What if the man put away his wife because of fornication? Then it is grammatically sound to say his remarriage was not adulterous. Why? Because the immorality, which broke his obligation to the marriage covenant, had already been committed

by the wife. She wasn't stoned, and thus removed from the picture, but this doesn't keep him bound. He has license to put away the adulterous wife, and to remarry just as if she were stoned. This is what Deut. 24 teaches – that a case of "nakedness" or immorality allows for divorce and remarriage without one mate being killed.

4. Jesus makes it clear that not every person has the ability to live in singleness. We will see Paul in I Cor. 7 backing this up. Those who teach the espousal theory ignore this basic principle of scripture, and have Jesus contradicting himself by: 1. Saying people have to remain single after divorce under all circumstances; and then 2. Saying not everyone can do this.

5. Divorce and remarriage is only called adultery when there is obligation for reconciliation and not sufficient reason to be separated. They are divorced, but they ought to be married. They have no right to be divorced, so they have no right to remarry. The person who is rightly and lawfully divorced has license to remarry without sin.

6. Notice that Jesus doesn't change the disciple's views on remarriage, but on divorce. The disciples are shocked that a man could not get rid of a woman just because she was displeasing. They had obviously been infected by the thought of the day. That thought being, that women were at the mercy of the men, who could put her away for "every cause". The Jewish men had come to look upon divorce as a gift of God to them.

■ SO, WHAT DID JESUS CHANGE?

Since the church is not the civil government as it was

in the Old Testament, stoning is not for the church. We must realize here that "stoning" was not in the Jew's power under the Roman government either. Jesus stamps his approval on divorce (and not just stoning) for sexual sin, and puts divorce for "every cause" in its proper light – adulterous. Jesus made it clear that to follow him means to live by what is righteous; not simply what is presently legal. Now we understand that to look lustfully is adultery. Now we know that to divorce or remarry unrighteously is classified as adultery. We know that hating our brother is having murder in our hearts. Monogamy has been restored as God's first will for marriage.

Jesus rightly interpreted and applied the moral law. He laid down the standard that His Kingdom is based on seeking right, not excusing wrong. Those who come into His Kingdom must repent of seeking to excuse their sin, and pursue God's will with all their hearts. In Christ's Kingdom, you can no longer have "hardness of heart", but must love your enemies and forgive those who repent (or not be forgiven). **In this light, and with this understanding, two believers cannot divorce, and still be "two believers".** To commit presumptuous sin can cut you off from God's mercy, and seal your doom. Don't tempt God. Divorce will only take place between believers if one becomes apostate – which is what happens when they turn to sin. (This also led to separation in the Old Testament - though by stoning -Deut. 13:6-11).

Christians are to seek what glorifies Christ. This sometimes includes divorce if your mate turns to immorality; and sometimes includes remarriage (for the brother/sister who doesn't have the gift to remain

77

single, and has been cleared from any obligation for reconciliation). After sin has been committed, it glorifies Christ for us to work through the biblical obligations with wisdom and carefulness to bring the situation to rest, and produce peace (I Cor. 7). If churches neglect their duty to help people work through their problems biblically, the problems only get worse -- and harder to unravel. God's Law is God's wisdom for bringing hard cases to rest.

It glorifies Christ for Christians who have been sinned against to forgive and restore the repentant sinner -- even if it is immorality in your mate. If God hadn't done this, you'd be lost forever without hope of salvation. Every time you yield to the flesh or lust after the things of the world, you commit spiritual adultery. Aren't you glad God forgives when you repent? In a Biblical church setting there is authority structure to help determine what to do — if reconciliation is possible or right, and the terms of reconciliation.

■ REVIEW

1. Jesus didn't teach contrary to Moses, or say that Moses made a mistake, but vindicated God's Law by showing the true intent of the Law, and the proper interpretation of "some uncleanness" or "matter of nakedness". These allowances were not permission to sin, but "what to do now" statutes, which were designed to resolve problems caused by people's mistakes and problems.
2. Jesus put his approval on divorce for sexual sin, instead of only stoning the offender.

3. Jesus made it clear that when divorce with a proper bill of divorce is for immorality, then remarriage is not adulterous.

4. Although Jesus reminded us of God's perfect ideal, He also recognized and endorsed the law (divorce for fornication), which deals with sinful mankind. We are to strive for the ideal; but when sin happens, we also need to know what righteous steps to take to bring the situation to rest.

5. Jesus made it clear that: Just because you've used a bill of divorce, adultery is still committed when you break up a marriage and start another on insufficient grounds. The only things that can break your obligation to the marriage covenant are death, immorality, and Paul adds apostasy (which is from the Old Testament also).

6. Jesus declares that not every person has the gift to stay content in the single state. NOTE: Some say these precepts only applied to the men, and that women could not divorce on similar grounds. However, Jesus spoke of men divorcing and women divorcing back-to-back in Mark 10. Paul speaks of this back-to-back in 1 Cor. 7:12-15. We know the Greeks and Romans allowed women to divorce men, and Adam Clarke states that it happened among the Jews also, according to history (See his note on I Cor. 7:11). This seems to indicate that if a husband was a transgressor of the law or apostate, she could divorce probably by making an appeal to the authorities. Polygamy was not sufficient grounds for divorce in the Old Testament, but apostasy and lack of support was, as we have given reference for already.

7. Some teach that the "exception clause" only applies to the divorce, but not the remarriage. Let me show you how this must be false:

   A. In order to actually say it their way, you'd have to say: "Whoever divorces his wife, except for fornication, commits adultery; and whoever divorces for fornication and then remarries commits adultery". This is the only way to say what they want Jesus' words to mean.

   B. These people believe: "Whoever divorces his wife for fornication and remarries commits adultery." Notice how this is opposite to what Jesus actually said, "Whosoever shall put away his wife, except it be for fornication, and shall marry another, committeth adultery."

   C. The way Jesus said it, the exception clause modifies ONE person doing TWO things (divorce & remarry), which resulted in adultery ONE TIME, unless the ONE person did the FIRST thing (divorce) for the "cause of fornication". The exception means the ONE person did not commit adultery ONE TIME when doing the TWO things. The Bible doesn't say that divorce alone is adultery. The exception clause takes you to a new situation with different rules — this is true for any exception with any law.

6

How Did Paul Understand Jesus?

It is very important to have an apostle, who fully knew the mind of Christ on such subjects as divorce and remarriage, to comment on the issue. The apostle's writings are Scripture just as when they penned Jesus' words – "*The black letters are just as important as the red ones.*

I Cor. 7:1-5,

"Now concerning the things whereof ye wrote unto me: It is good for a man not to touch a woman. Nevertheless, to avoid fornication, let every man have his own wife, and let every woman have her own husband. Let the husband render unto the wife due benevolence: and likewise also the wife unto the husband. The wife hath not power of her own body, but the husband: and likewise also the husband hath not power of his own body, but the wife. Defraud ye not one the other, except it be with consent for a time, that ye may give yourselves

to fasting and prayer; and come together again, that Satan tempt you not for your incontinency."

True faith will never ask, "what can I get by with?"; but "what will glorify Christ?" We are bound to live by a striving, obedient faith, not just fit within a law. Paul here is speaking of glorifying Christ.

1. It is good to be single, and serve Christ without distraction. This is mentioned many times in this chapter. The early Christians put high regard on "virginity for Jesus' sake". Jesus himself said, "He that is able to receive it, let him receive it." Jesus and Paul declare that this ability is a gift of God, and not to be forced on people by church leaders (Matt. 19:11; I Cor. 7).

2. Because all cannot receive this single state (at least not yet); Paul says they should marry, so they aren't drawn into fornication by their inability to control their natural passions and weaknesses. This will also be repeated, and is important to remember concerning those divorced with no chance of reconciliation.

3. Paul did not say, "Let every man have his first wife". How would this be a remedy for potential fornication to those whose first mate was married to someone else, was an unbeliever, or didn't want them? Obviously, if God doesn't open the doors for marriage He will sustain a person until he does. This is no excuse for fornication, but a principle that the Holy Spirit wanted church leaders to be aware of so they wouldn't make the mistake of forced singleness. A person CAN remain pure until God opens the door for

marriage; but if leaders force people to be single against their own faith and will, grave consequences will result.

4. Once married, you must strive to meet your mate's needs, and only abstain with consent for a short time of prayer and fasting. This principle is neglected by those who teach this "separation, but not divorce" principle. This doesn't resolve the problem, but makes it worse. A person who separates, but doesn't divorce, needs to seek reconciliation or is disobeying God. Only lawful divorce or death frees you from this duty.

5. Single people need to listen close: Either you marry, or you keep your hands off. This is God's options for you. Hands - off courtship is God's plan.

I Cor. 7:6-9,

"But I speak this by permission, and not of commandment. For I would that all men were even as I myself. But every man hath his proper gift of God, one after this manner, and another after that. I say therefore to the unmarried and widows, It is good for them if they abide even as I. But if they cannot contain, let them marry: for it is better to marry than to burn."

Paul stresses again his desire that people give themselves totally to God without the distraction of marriage; but again, he says this must be according to the gift of God. Men must not tell people, **"you have to contain"**; when God says, **"If they cannot contain, let them marry"**. Notice how many times "Let" is

83

used in this chapter. We must "let" when God says "let", or we will cause people to fall into fornication and burning. In all this chapter, Paul never says, "God only accepts first marriages", or anything like it! When he says to let every person have their own wife/husband; let them render due benevolence; let them marry, etc. he never specifies, "only if it is a first marriage".

Some might object that Paul is speaking only to single men and widows, not divorced women. Can you prove that? He didn't say, "virgins and widows". Would Paul recognize a young widow's inability to remain content and pure in a single state for the rest of her life; yet tell a young divorced woman (without hope of reconciliation due to her husband's remarriage) to just "tough it"? Doesn't he say in verse 15 of this chapter that a brother or a sister is not under bondage in such cases?

Truly, the only time a Christian woman will be divorced without hope of reconciliation is when the unbeliever departs. For even if she was married to a believer, yet for him to divorce and remarry contrary to Scripture would also be his apostasy from God, would result in excommunication, and leave us to treat him as an heathen man (Matt. 18:17).

It is important to note at this point that widows in the Scriptures seem to include deserted brides or divorced women as well: See Isaiah 54:4-7: (also 2 Sam. 20:3)

"...for thou shalt forget the shame of thy youth, and shalt not remember the reproach of thy widowhood

any more...For the LORD hath called thee as a woman forsaken and grieved in spirit, and a wife of youth, when thou wast refused, saith thy God. For a small moment have I forsaken thee; but with great mercies will I gather thee." Isaiah 54:4-7

I believe that a woman whose circumstances have left them without obligation to reconcile a marriage are then considered widows, and not just a "divorced woman" as in the context of Jesus' words in Matt 5 & 19 where reconciliation is an obligation, thus making the marriage to another adultery against the first marriage covenant.

Many laws concerning widows in the Old Testament and New Testament must include divorced women with no hope of reconciliation as well -- they are technically the same, and they have the same needs and problems. Paul says in **I Timothy 5: 14, "I will therefore that the younger [widows] marry, bear children, guide the house, give none occasion to the adversary to speak reproachfully".** This solution to a potential problem in the church would need to apply to young deserted wives with no hope of reconciliation as well. They would have the same problems and dangers. This situation was probably dealt with case by case according to the counsel of the bishops and elders. Origen, while writing against allowing divorce and remarriage, tells us that church leaders (plural) in his day were allowing some divorced women to remarry. Since the Romish church tended to destroy and suppress what didn't agree with it, we don't have the writings of these people, if they even left any. Here are Origen's Words though:

"But now contrary to what is written, even some of the rulers of the church have permitted a woman to marry, even when her husband was living, doing contrary to what was written. For it is said, A wife is bound so long as her husband lives." Origen (c. 245)

Notice that Origen skipped the portion of the verse that says she is bound "by the Law"; because this surrenders the case for him. The Law Paul is referring to is Moses' Law, and this law allowed for divorce and remarriage.

I Cor. 7:10-11,

"And unto the married I command, yet not I, but the Lord, Let not the wife depart from her husband: but and if she depart, let her remain unmarried, or be reconciled to her husband: and let not the husband put away his wife."

DON'T MISS THIS. Paul is giving his understanding of Jesus' words here. This is Jesus' law of marriage for two believers.

1. It refers to two married believers (Jesus was preaching to covenant Jews, not Gentiles; and Paul is speaking to believers).

2. Believers are not to divorce & remarry; but to work through their problems and be victorious in Christ.

3. If separation happens, the next step must be reconciliation; and as long as reconciliation is possible, then remarriage is forbidden.

4. In the next verses Paul deals with what happens

when one mate in this scenario becomes apostate. Though Paul (in vss. 12-15) is also dealing with those who come to Christ while married to a lost person; the principles for mixed marriages still apply to a person married to one who is excommunicated. When one turns to fornication or apostasy from Christ, the other mate is not bound to the marriage covenant - thus not bound to remain single for reconciliation if divorce occurs.

Those who teach that divorced people are "still married in God's eyes", unwittingly set people up for sin and confusion. If they are divorced, but still married in "God's eyes"; can they resume sexual relations? Do they need to remarry? Many times church leaders will tell remarried people they are really still married to the first mate -- so is this polygamy or polyandry? The Bible says the unlawfully divorced person is unmarried but obligated to reconcile.

This passage has to do with regulating believers, as the church doesn't "judge them that are without" (I Cor. 5:12,13). So if a believer initiates a divorce, because of incompatibility, they must remain unmarried in order to reconcile.

I Cor. 7:12-16,

"But to the rest speak I, not the Lord: If any brother hath a wife that believeth not, and she be pleased to dwell with him, let him not put her away. And the woman which hath an husband that believeth not, and if he be pleased to dwell with her, let her not leave him. For the unbelieving husband is sanctified

87

by the wife, and the unbelieving wife is sanctified by the husband: else were your children unclean; but now are they holy. But if the unbelieving depart, let him depart. A brother or a sister is not under bondage in such cases: but God hath called us to peace. For what knowest thou, O wife, whether thou shalt save thy husband? or how knowest thou, O man, whether thou shalt save thy wife?"

1. **"To the rest speak I, not the Lord"**; is simply Paul's way of telling us that he is going to cover a situation that Jesus didn't cover while teaching on earth. **Jesus' words were not meant to cover every situation.** This situation is: "What if the unbeliever divorces a believer?" The believer is not allowed to divorce, except for immorality, which in the church would bring discipline. If they have presumptuously separated, they must remain single until they can be reconciled. But if the unbeliever doesn't want to remain married to his/her converted Christian mate, and they file for divorce; the believer is to allow the divorce, and is not sinning in this divorce. The sin of unlawful divorce is on the head of the unbeliever. Paul says this is a different situation, not covered by Christ's words.

2. **The believer is not to compromise their obedience to Christ, or forsake Christ for the unbeliever.** If they are not pleased to dwell with you while you follow Jesus, let them depart. This is part of loving Jesus more than husband, wife, mother, father, son, daughter, and your own life. I Peter 3 makes this very clear in regards to dress and conduct. The wife should please the Lord, even if she loses her husband. You should also read I Peter 2:18-24. Of course, the goal is

not to drive the unbeliever away, but to win them to Christ. A believer sins unless they do all in their power (within the Law of Christ) to win their lost mate and not drive him away.

3. Notice what God's solutions strive to produce in the home: PEACE. God doesn't split up marriages in the New Testament, even when he did in the Old. In Nehemiah's case they didn't seem to care about the unbelieving mate and children's salvation; but in the New Testament, we hold the home together for the sake of winning the lost, and for the children! We also don't force people to be single, who have not the gift to do so.

4. Notice the difference between *bound* and *loosed* in this chapter. When you are *loosed* you are **not** *bound,* and when you are *bound*, you are **not** *loosed.* When you are *loosed*, you can remarry without sin (7:28). Divorced doesn't always mean *loosed,* if you are divorced with obligation to reconcile. These people who were divorced by unbelievers, should still seek to win their mate; but really aren't bound to the obligation of reconciliation, unless there is repentance -- now not only repentance about the divorce, but concerning their attitude toward Christ, as the believer cannot marry an unbeliever. Reconciliation is not in the believer's power, but the unbeliever's; and the church cannot regulate unbelievers that are outside the body.

So, does God automatically give the forsaken believer the gift of singleness? Some say so, but I don't see it anywhere. If the unbeliever remarries, there is absolutely no hope of reconciliation. Should they then be forced to be single? Doesn't Paul say this can cause fornication or burning? *"If they cannot contain, let them marry"*. You cannot deny your church members the allowance for weakness unless Paul did - - he didn't. **"If they cannot contain, let them marry"** is a command.

5. The fact that Paul says the brother or sister in this case is **"not under bondage"** is set as a contrast to the last case he presented: **"But if the woman depart, let her remain unmarried, or be reconciled to her husband"**. She was still bound by the law to her obligation of reconciliation, because she (a believer) had initiated an unlawful divorce or separation. The case presented in vss. 12-15 is set in contrast to the situation in vss. 10 & 11. The first situation was a marriage of professed believers, which Paul says is what Jesus had taught about (He was speaking to covenant Jews, not Gentiles); the second situation was an unequal yoke between a believer and an unbeliever, which Paul says Jesus didn't discuss. In the first situation, the parties are bound to reconcile; but in the second situation the parties are said to be "not bound".

There would be no difference in the two situations and no contrast, if "not bound" still left them bound to "remain unmarried or reconcile". The first woman departed while under the command not to depart. The second woman let the unbeliever depart according to the command, "let him depart". The first woman was not lawfully loosed; but the second woman was lawfully loosed. The same principle obviously applied to the men as well.

90

Adam Clarke, admitting the law in his day wasn't biblical on this subject, says concerning this verse, "..a Christian man or woman, is not under bondage to any particular laws, so as to be prevented from remarrying. Such, probably, the law stood then; but it is not so now; for the marriage can only be dissolved by death, or the the ecclesiastical court."

I would recommend a believer, in this situation of being divorced by an unbeliever, to remain single for a while and pray for the other's salvation and reconciliation until the unbeliever dies, persists in immorality, or remarries. This keeps the door open for repentance and reconciliation.

Someone will argue: "Jesus said it was adultery to marry a divorced woman! He didn't say it was only a sin if she was still under obligation to reconcile!" That is a good point, but let me ask you: "If a woman is divorced by her husband, and a month later the man dies; isn't she still a 'divorced woman'? Did Jesus say, 'It is adultery to marry a divorced woman until her husband dies'? He didn't say that either, but you assume that from other Scriptures, right? I could argue that, because he didn't say that, she could never get married, even if her ex-husband dies - if I were to follow your type of exegesis. It seems obvious that Jesus is speaking of the woman divorced in that unlawful scenario; not every divorced woman everywhere for every reason.

I believe it is sinful to marry her, because she is under obligation to reconcile. Whether her husband dies or remarries, that obligation dies, because it becomes impossible to reconcile. Thus, from looking at the whole picture, I believe she, though divorced, was able to remarry without sin once her obligation to the first marriage covenant was destroyed, whether by death, apostasy, immorality, or the man's remarriage. This I believe God made clear in Deut. 24:4; Jesus made clear in Matthew 19:9; and Paul did in I Cor. 7:15.

Some say it is best to play it safe, and not to allow the divorced woman to ever remarry. I question whether that is really the safe position to take, in light of Paul's teaching not to force singleness on people. Is it safer to be in marriage, or in burning? Do we want a divorced woman, who can't marry, and may be burning for companionship, in our church? Is that safe? Paul said, "To avoid fornication, let every man have his own wife; and let every woman have her own husband." A woman who cannot be reconciled to her former husband is in the same state as the widow, whom Paul says should marry (I Tim. 5:11; I Cor. 7:9); and is not under bondage I Cor. 7:15. She is not "bound by the law" to a husband, because no man is her husband.

I Cor. 7:17-28,

"But as God hath distributed to every man, as the Lord hath called every one, so let him walk. And so ordain I in all churches. Is any man called being circumcised? let him not become uncircumcised. Is any called in uncircumcision? let him not be circumcised.   Circumcision   is   nothing,   and uncircumcision is nothing, but the keeping of the commandments of God. Let every man abide in the same calling wherein he was called. Art thou called

being a servant? care not for it: but if thou mayest be made free, use it rather. For he that is called in the Lord, being a servant, is the Lord's freeman: likewise also he that is called, being free, is Christ's servant. Ye are bought with a price; be not ye the servants of men. Brethren, let every man wherein he is called, therein abide with God. Now concerning virgins I have no commandment of the Lord: yet I give my judgment, as one that hath obtained mercy of the Lord to be faithful. I suppose therefore that this is good for the present distress, I say, that it is good for a man so to be. Art thou bound unto a wife? seek not to be loosed. Art thou loosed from a wife? seek not a wife. But and if thou marry, thou hast not sinned; and if a virgin marry, she hath not sinned. Nevertheless such shall have trouble in the flesh: but I spare you."

Three times Paul says to allow people to remain in the same circumstance wherein they are called. I have a tract that tries to say this only refers to circumcision or servant-hood, as though Paul is so senile that he changes subjects midstream, and then jumps back on track! Paul is speaking about MARRIAGE, but using circumcision and servant-hood as examples, just as he uses the woman's hair to illustrate the teaching on head veils.

If you are married to an unbeliever, stay married. If you are in a second marriage, stay married. If you are loosed from a wife, don't seek one; but if you marry, you haven't sinned. Paul says that even in that time of "distress" and persecution, when it was not advisable to marry at all; yet it was not sin for a divorced (loosed) man to remarry. "Loosed" must

93

mean the same in both places — it cannot mean "by death", as no one would "seek to be loosed" by this method, being a Christian.

"Let every man abide in the same calling wherein he is called...." Even if you could prove Christians cannot divorce or remarry under any circumstance, this principle would still demand that you accept converts already in this situation. One man told me that to accept remarried people was the same as accepting two homosexuals living together. This is simply unacceptable! What if Paul started preaching such nonsense in the first century to remarried Jews? Talk about a riot!! It is sad when people won't think their theology back into the first century. Our faith and practice should be the same as theirs. God chose to allow divorce and remarriage, but never homosexuality.

If Paul was against second marriages as much as many are today, you know he would have spent half this chapter (I Cor. 7) on that subject. When he said the believer, who was left by the unbeliever, wasn't bound; he would have made sure we knew they couldn't remarry -- especially in the light of verses 27, and 28. But, we can see he didn't. Paul did emphasize the superiority of singleness more than many today. I don't believe this was only for the present distress. We should lift up this as an honorable lifestyle, rather than whisper about the poor fellow or old maid, who never found anyone. Paul says those single for Jesus' sake are stronger and sometimes more useful than us married folks. When Jesus said, "he that can receive it, let him receive it", he wasn't talking about the "present distress".

Paul did indicate that it was good for a bishop or deacon to be married (to one wife). I believe this is for two reasons:

1. When you are leading men and women, it is good to have a wife to protect you from temptation and false accusation.

2. Your qualification for leading a church is seen in your ability to lead your home and family.

I Tim. 5:11-14

"But the younger widows refuse: for when they have begun to wax wanton against Christ, they will marry; having damnation, because they have cast off their first faith. And withal they learn to be idle, wandering about from house to house; and not only idle, but tattlers also and busybodies, speaking things which they ought not. I will therefore that the younger women marry, bear children, guide the house, give none occasion to the adversary to speak reproachfully."

Somehow I don't see any difference in this wise judgment being said for young widows or young divorced women, who have no hope of reconciliation.

7

Facts We Must Face

"We then that are strong ought to bear the infirmities of the weak, and not to please ourselves. Let every one of us please his neighbor for his good to edification. For even Christ pleased not himself; but, as it is written, The reproaches of them that reproached thee are fallen upon me." Romans 15:1-3

"For he shall have judgment without mercy, that hath showed no mercy; and mercy rejoiceth against judgment." James 2:13

Whether we like it or not, Christ's Church is made up of PEOPLE: People with a past; people who sin; people who have weaknesses; people who fall down; and people who become apostates, and leave their families with needs. Church leaders must be willing to Biblically work people through their problems. Jesus did not eradicate the ability to sin from believers, and not all believers are mature. Not all believers come in a nice package; but many have a messed up past.

Jesus was not ashamed to call repentant believers BRETHREN, no matter what their past condition.

If we take the publicans, harlots, and remarried people when they repent: If we love them and help them through their problems; we will be reproached for befriending "publicans and sinners" -- "the reproaches of them that reproached thee are fallen upon me". This is what happened to Jesus when he accepted and loved YOU! He called you a brother; and got reproached with, "HE is your brother?" "Your a friend of sinners!" Jesus answered with, "They that be whole don't need a physician, but they that are sick." We must receive repentant people where they are, and bring them to maturity. We must discipline the rebellious. We must not condone sinful practices, but must deal with them as the apostles did. Being in Christ's Kingdom doesn't guarantee your spouse won't leave you and go into sin. Being a Biblical Church doesn't mean there will be no weak brothers or sisters. But, being a Biblical Church will help keep insincere people from joining. Having proper discipline and standards will be a preventive medicine against sin in the church. If we, individually, stay on fire for Christ, and pray for each other; the weak won't fall, but become strong.

Divorce and remarriage always leaves a question mark over a person's character and ability to lead their home. 99% of the time when there is divorce, there is some fault on both sides. Many people have an uneasy conscience about remarried people, because of the controversial aspect of the issue. This is why bishops and deacons should be free from this stigma (I Tim. 3; Titus 1:5-9). "Husband of one wife" doesn't necessarily refer to marrying after your mate dies; but to polygamy or a failed home (divorce and remarriage).

In the law it is forbidden to a priest to marry a harlot, a foreigner, a widow or a divorced woman, because he is a special case (Lev. 21:7,13,14; Ez. 44:22). Other men could do this without sin (if the woman was free from obligation). Remember Boaz's mother was Rahab "the harlot". Listen to Christ's lineage in Matthew, "And Salmon begat Boaz of Rahab (the harlot foreigner); and Boaz begat Obed of Ruth (a widow foreigner); and Obed begat Jesse; and Jesse begat David the king; and David the king begat Solomon of her that had been the wife of Urias (Bathsheba: an adulterous widow)" What priests could not do, others could. In the Old Testament a widow and a divorced woman seemed to be looked upon in much the same way (see also Lev. 22:13 and Num. 30:9).

In about 390 A.D. The Apostolic Constitutions were compiled. These were not written by the apostles, but were beliefs of the early church in the third century and maybe earlier. These constitutions use the same precept (mentioned above) for ministers in the following words: "He who has taken a widow, or a divorced woman, or an harlot, or a servant, or one belonging to the theatre, cannot be either a bishop, priest, or deacon, or indeed any one of the sacerdotal catalogue" (Book 8) And again in book 6, "But we do not permit any one of the clergy to take to wife either a courtesan, or a servant, or a widow, or one that is divorced, as also the law says." Now, this would mean nothing if other men could not do this. But we know that other men could marry a widow, a converted harlot, a lawfully divorced woman, a servant, a converted actress, etc. The whole idea is that a priest (Old Testament) or a bishop (New Testament) could not do this, because they were special.

It cannot be denied that the early church discerned between what happened before you were baptized, and what happened after you were baptized. There were differences of opinion on other issues; **but no trace of the policy of making new converts divorce if they were on a second marriage.**

Some have said, "What if one of our youth run off, marry a divorced person, and want to come back; shall we receive them back? Would you rather they not repent and want to come back? What did the father do when his prodigal son wanted to come back? It is hard to deal with people "after the fact"; but we must!!

The church is a hospital for repentant sinners, not an elite club for mature saints. He that is without sin among you, let him be the first to bar those with a past from the church; when neither Jesus, nor the apostles did.

In Peter Allix's The Ecclesiastical History of the Ancient Churches of Piedmont and of the Albigences, he states about St. Chromatius (one of those who never supported papal dominion), that, **"He plainly asserts, that marriage is so wholly dissolved by adultery, that it is lawful for the innocent party to marry again".** This Allix says was also, **"...the opinion of the Romish Church till after the tenth century."** This shows agreement on this subject between Roman Catholics and the faithful dissenters in the fifth century and (according to Allix) until the tenth century. Philip Schaff, in his History of the Christian Church also shows the church allowing divorce only in the case of adultery until near the tenth century. Remember that Origen is quoted earlier as complaining that church leaders were allowing divorced women to remarry in some cases.

Though there have always been some extremists on this issue, yet, I believe our position has been rather commonly held. Menno Simons (Anabaptist leader), and protestants, in general, held this position during the reformation.

Let us hear what Menno Simons (a prominent leader of the most conservative and biblical group during reformation times) has to say about divorce and remarriage due to immorality or the unbelieving one departing. (Complete Writings):

"We acknowledge, teach, and assent to no other marriage than that which Christ and His apostles publicly and plainly taught in the New Testament, namely, of one man and one woman (Matt. 19:4), and that they may not be divorced except in case of adultery (Matt. 5:32); for the two are one flesh, but if the unbelieving one depart, a sister or brother is not under bondage in that case. I Cor. 7:15." pg. 200

"For divorce is not allowed by the Scriptures except for adultery." pg.479

"These two, one husband and one wife, are one flesh and can not be separated from each other to marry again otherwise than for adultery, as the Lord says. Matt. 5:19; Mark 10; Luke 16." pg. 561

"We know too that the bond of undefiled, honorable matrimony is so firm and fast in the kingdom and government of Christ, that no man may leave his wife, nor a wife her husband, and marry another (understand rightly what Christ says), except it be for adultery. Paul also holds the same doctrine that they shall be so bound to each other that the man has not power over his own body, nor the woman over hers." pg.970

Notice that Menno is not sheepishly defending what he considers the liberal view, but speaking with earnest about the strength of the marriage bond.

Now listen to Menno on the matter of past sin in one's life. This is about those who have "shacked up" unmarried, and then left and later married another. The law says they should have married the one they first violated, but what about when it is already done in the past?

"I do not mean to say that a person who has in days gone by ignorantly done this thing must leave the wife whom he afterwards married and take in her stead the violated one. Not at all, for I doubt not but that the merciful Father will graciously overlook the errors of those who have ignorantly committed them, and who will now fear and gladly do what is right." pg. 379

Let us hear Menno once again on the matter of human weakness and resorting to marriage, rather than falling into sin.

"I write it that they may no more defile the bed of their neighbor nor violate young women, but live in all honor, each with his own wife; the unmarried keeping free from all immorality, and if he cannot restrain himself, let him seek a good pious wife in the fear of God." pg. 380

Many today feel the espousal theory is the "old paths" and allowing remarried people into the church is "going liberal"; but this is a false fear, based on a short sighted view of history. The Roman Catholics stopped allowing divorce sometime after the tenth century, but the reformers returned to the position I have presented (divorce and remarriage of the innocent party allowed for immorality).

Menno Simons, Dirk Philips, Leonard Bouwens, Gillis of Aachen, and three other Anabaptist leaders made this statement in 1554:

"If an unbeliever wishes to separate for reasons of the faith, then the believer shall conduct himself honestly. He shall not marry again as long as the unbeliever remains unmarried. But if the unbeliever marries or commits adultery, then the believing mate may also marry, subject to the advice of the elders of the congregation..."

In 1571, Anabaptist leader, Rauff Bisch said:

"We believe that nothing may terminate a marriage except adultery. But if the unbelieving wants to

divorce because of the faith, we would let him go as Paul says in I Cor. 7. We believe that the cause for divorce should never be found in the believer."

On page 401 in the Martyr's Mirror we find in an early Anabaptist confession of faith these words:

"...Christ the perfect Lawgiver...referring all that heard and believed him to the original ordinance of his heavenly Father...and thus re-establishing marriage between one man and one woman, and so inseparably and firmly binding the bond of matrimony, that they might not, on any account, separate and marry another, except in case of adultery or death."

Many of the Anabaptist leaders could read the Greek, Latin, German, and sometimes Hebrew. Many were well read and studied men; having access to the early church writings, and apocryphal writings. They believed in divorce and remarriage in the case of immorality. They gave their life for proper interpretations of Scripture. It wasn't until later years (near 1800) that many Mennonites changed to the "absolute no divorce, no remarriage" stand. While they were on fire and turning the world upside down, they believed as I've stated.

According to their own writings, much fewer could read Greek, Hebrew, and Latin in 1800 than could in the 1500's and 1600's. The early leaders had been trained in the universities, but they didn't want their children under that influence (and persecution didn't permit it), so the later generations didn't have the education of their fathers.

103

8

Important Questions To Answer

These have already been answered to some degree, but we will deal more in depth with them here

■ WHAT ABOUT ROMANS 7?

Romans 7:1-3 leads some to push the idea that remarried people are adulterers; but this wrests the scripture out of context twice. Paul is speaking in reference to Moses' Law as an illustration.

1. **He is speaking about Moses' law** ("I speak to them that know the law"). According to Moses' Law the woman was only called an adulteress if she was not divorced when she left. Notice the verse says, "For the woman which hath an husband is bound by the law to her husband so long as he liveth;". My house is mine by the law as long as I live; but that same law gives me the right to sell it. The wife is bound by the law; but that same law makes provisions for divorce also. A lawfully divorced woman has no husband, and so is not bound. Moses' Law calls him her "former

husband".

2.   In Romans 7, Paul is only using marriage as an illustration of the Law's bond upon us before our flesh (old man) died and we were remarried to Christ. We were the servants (wives) of sin, but became the servants (wives) of righteousness (Christ) (Romans 6). We were under the Law's jurisdiction and condemnation while married to the "old man". Our "flesh" was the occasion of the Law's hold upon us, just like a husband is the occasion of the Law's bond upon a woman. But if that husband is dead, that bond is broken. We could be rightly married to Christ because our flesh was put to death – crucified, renounced, etc. Thus freed from the law, we could be married or joined to Christ. This definitely means the woman in the illustration was not divorced when called an adulteress for leaving her husband for another man. This is consistent with Moses' Law, which Paul is speaking of.

■ WHY WASN'T THE EXCEPTION CLAUSE USED IN MARK AND LUKE?

Those who believe the espousal theory lay great stress upon the fact that in Mark 10:2-12 and Luke 16:18 Jesus doesn't mention the exception clause. They say this is because the Gentiles didn't have the espousal customs of the Jews, and since Matthew was written to the Jews, it is included. Mark and Luke were written to the Gentiles; therefore they didn't get the exception clause. They say this proves that the exception clause refers to the espousal, not marriage.

We have already showed that general rules are often

spoken without the exceptions included, and that the absence of exceptions spoken, do not mean there are none. Jesus is preaching against the general abuse of Moses' Law and saying, *Whoever puts away his wife so he can get another is committing adultery through legal channels, and whoever marries the woman thus put away is engaging in the adultery.*

There are a number of problems with this theory:

1. Jesus, in every instance, is speaking to Jews, not Gentiles. Are we to conclude that Mark and Luke are guilty of editing Jesus' words, rather than faithfully reporting them? Why didn't they edit out all references to the Sabbath, sacrifices in the temple, circumcision, and all other non-Gentile practices? Why don't we Gentiles deny the things found in Luke, but absent in Matthew? The Greek Matthew was most likely also written by Matthew, and the exception is still included.

Do they suppose the churches had separate services where only Jews heard Matthew, and Gentiles read Mark and Luke? Do they suppose Jews who lived in Rome could not put away an unfaithful espoused bride because they had Mark and not Matthew? Do they suppose Gentiles couldn't put away an engaged bride just because they had a different practice? Do they suppose Gentiles could "swear" because they had Mark and Luke, but not Matthew? Do they suppose the ones who read Mark didn't have to "turn the other cheek"? This type of thinking on their part leads to much foolishness.

2. There were Jews in every nation where Mark's and

Luke's Gospels were sent. The Gospel was to the Jew first, and also to the Gentile, even with Paul's approach to every new Gentile city – he started in the local synagogue. Also, the four Gospels were circulated throughout all the churches very early. The early Christians saw no discrepancy in this. Why? Because, like in any other situation, the synoptic Gospels (Matt., Mark, and Luke) supply the missing links to the other Gospels. We don't subtract the differences, we add them. The different accounts compliment each other, not contradict or take away.

3. The argument about the lawfulness of divorce was over the abuse of Deut. 24 (divorce for "every cause"; not divorce in case of immorality). Divorce for immorality was commonly understood, so Jesus didn't have to mention that exception clause every time. When the apostles tell us, "submit yourself to every ordinance of man," or "obey them that have the rule over you," or "wives obey your husbands"; do we take these to be without exceptions? They don't give any exceptions! But we know that in other places there are obvious exceptions. What if they had mentioned these same commands in another place with an exception? Wouldn't we understand there to be an exception for the other times when they didn't mention the exception? Of course we would! It is not necessary to always mention every exception when stating a general rule. Many times exceptions are understood, but not mentioned, because the person is not dealing with the exceptions (as in Romans 7). Paul even tells us, as we will later discuss, that Jesus' words didn't cover every situation, because he says, "To the rest speak I, not the Lord" (I Cor. 7).

107

4. In Matthew they asked if divorce *for every cause* was lawful, which is why Jesus told them what *cause* was lawful (fornication). In Mark they asked if *divorce* was lawful. Jesus simply pointed them to Genesis as God's intent, and away from Duet. 24 (Their supposed loophole). Later, in the house, he told the disciples what he also said in Luke: *To put away your mate for the express reason of getting another is adulterous, and an abuse of God's Law.* In Mark He makes it clear that the crime of adultery was against the first wife, not just in the taking of another – polygamy would not be called adultery, but the violation of duty to the first wife made it adulterous. In Luke, Jesus mentions the divorce and remarriage situation immediately after saying, "...it is easier for heaven and earth to pass, than one tittle of the law to fail." This means his words in verse 18 were just his proper interpretation of the law in light of the contemporary controversy over Duet. 24! He then goes on to tell the rich man in hell that his brothers can only be saved by "hearing Moses and the prophets".

5. Tertullian (160-230 AD), a Gentile Christian, who is faulted with being radically strict in the area of marriage, said this of the words of Christ when contending with Marcion (a heretic who taught the creator was an evil God, and not the Father of Jesus):

"But, observe, if this Christ be yours when he teaches contrary to Moses and the Creator, on the same principle must He be mine if I can show that His teaching is not contrary to them. I maintain, then, that there was a condition in the prohibition which he now made of divorce; the case supposed being,

that a man put away his wife for the express purpose of marrying another. His words are: "Whosoever putteth away his wife, and marrieth another, committeth adultery; and whosoever marrieth her that is put away from her husband, also committeth adultery," -- "put away," that is, for the reason wherefore a woman ought not to be dismissed, that another wife may be obtained. For he who marries a woman who is unlawfully put away is as much of an adulterer as the man who marries one who is undivorced. Permanent is the marriage which is not rightly dissolved; to marry, therefore, whilst matrimony is undissolved, is to commit adultery. Since, therefore, His prohibition of divorce was a conditional one, He did not prohibit absolutely; and what He did not absolutely forbid, that He permitted on some occasions, when there is an absence of the cause why He gave the prohibition. In very deed His teaching is not contrary to Moses, whose precept he partially defends, I will not say confirms. If, however, you deny that divorce is in any way permitted by Christ, how is it that you on your side destroy marriage, not uniting man and woman, nor admitting to the sacrament of baptism and of the eucharist those who have been united in marriage anywhere else, unless they should agree together to repudiate the fruit of their marriage, and so the very Creator Himself? Well, then, what is a husband to do in your sect, if his wife commit adultery? Shall he keep her? But your own apostle, you know, does not permit "the members of Christ to be joined to a harlot." Divorce, therefore, when justly deserved, has even in Christ a defender. So that Moses for the future must be considered as being confirmed by

Him, since he allows divorce in the same sense as Christ does, if any unchastity should occur in the wife. For in the Gospel of Matthew he says, "Whosoever shall put away his wife, saving for the cause of fornication, causeth her to commit adultery." ...The Creator, however, except on account of adultery, does not put asunder what He Himself joined together....He prohibits divorce when He will have the marriage inviolable; he permits divorce when the marriage is spotted with unfaithfulness." Tertullian 3.404,405

Notice: Tertullian didn't even mention the espousal theory; he understood the exception clause to mean unchastity (immorality) and adultery; he understood Christ wasn't changing Moses; he believed the adultery of remarriage was due to "unlawful divorce"; he didn't believe in a separation short of divorce; and he had the Gospel of Matthew in Africa. This doesn't mean I agree with Tertullian in all areas, but that, even in his extremist views, he still admits what I am stating. Later, he went so far as to say that even a widow remarrying was wrong.

■ WHAT DOES "FORNICATION" MEAN?

Some will contend that fornication only refers to sexual relations between unmarried people, and therefore Jesus can only be speaking of sexual sin before marriage -- the betrothal or espousal theory. However, these same people, not thinking far enough, won't allow divorce and remarriage if one learns during marriage that their mate was unfaithful before the marriage. They still call a marriage an *unbreakable* "one flesh" union, even if there was fornication before the wedding; but Paul says that one joined to a harlot (fornication) produces a "one flesh" union, and God's Law says they should have married the one they first violated. This causes great problems with their interpretation.

The early church writings knew nothing of such an espousal theory, and always mentioned the exception clause as referring to the immorality of married people. The whole context of the Pharisees' question is married people. They are referring to Deut. 24, which is speaking of married people, not engagement. Deut. 24 gave the reason for lawful divorce as "some uncleanness" or "matter of nakedness", which I believe corresponds with Jesus' use of fornication or immorality as the proper interpretation of Deut. 24.

It is sad that people wreck homes and bar people from the church because they read an "American Law" definition of an "English" word back into the scripture. In American law, the word fornication has come to mean sexual sin between single people, while adultery means sexual sin of married people. But this is not the usage in the Old or New Testaments; early church writings; or apocryphal writings.

The Scriptural usage of fornication (porneia) is immorality in general, harlotry. Some use adultery and fornication interchangeably, but this is not always accurate. Fornication refers to the act of sin, while adultery has the violation of the marriage covenant in view, which is done by the act of fornication. Adultery is the RESULT of fornication. In Sirach 23:22,24, this is said about an unfaithful wife: "...en porneia

111

emoicheuthe" ("she committed adultery by fornication"). By partaking in sexual sin, they violate the marriage covenant.

William Tyndale's translation, rather than using the word "adultery" he used "breaketh wedlock", or "commits advoutry" (breaks vows). This shows the meaning of the word adultery to refer to the breaking of the marriage covenant.

Rev. 2:20-23

"...thou sufferest that woman Jezebel, which calleth herself a prophetess, to teach and to seduce my servants to commit fornication, ...I gave her space to repent of her fornication;...I will cast her into a bed, and them that commit adultery with her into great tribulation...And I will kill her children...."

Does God know how to use these terms in the correct fashion? They committed adultery by fornication. She committed adultery and fornication; and she had children.

See I Cor. 10:18 where 23,000 people are killed for fornication -- were all these unmarried? In Acts 15 the apostles decided what parts of the Mosaic Law should be expected of the Gentiles. They wrote to the churches thus: "...That ye abstain from meats offered to idols, and from blood, and from things strangled, and from fornication:" Do we suppose this included adultery? Yes, it actually included all the immorality associated with their past idolatry. Compare the list of three sins in Eph. 5:3 with the same list in Eph. 5:5. You will notice that "fornication" is interchangeable with "whoremonger".

The Bible uses fornication for incest (I Cor. 5), homosexuality (Jude 7), and adultery (Jer. 3:1-8, where the adulteress is divorced for her fornication/whoredom/harlotry; the Hebrew word for fornication is "zana"). See also the use of porneia in the Septuagint in Ezek. 16:22; Hosea 2:2,5; Amos 7:17, etc. God espoused Israel to himself from Egypt (Jer. 2:1-3; Ezek. 16:8), but she committed fornication (Ezek. 16:20,26,32,38-40) and was thus put away (Hosea 2:2; Isa. 50:1; Jer. 3:8,20;) Notice how God plans to stone Israel (Ezek. 16:40) in his fury; but then we see him represented as using the bill of divorce by another prophet (Jer. 3:8). It is clear these were for a wife who committed adultery (Ezek. 16:32) by fornication (Ezek. 16:26).

Those who teach the espousal theory tell us that if you find out your new bride committed sexual sin yesterday (before the wedding) you can divorce her and marry another without sin; but if she commits sexual sin tomorrow you have to keep her. Truly, according to Jesus' words (if we make fornication only premarital sexual sin) you can divorce your wife after five or ten years of marriage, as long as you find out she sinned before the wedding. Erroneous doctrine always causes problems it cannot solve

■ DO SECOND MARRIAGES = ADULTEROUS AFFAIRS?

"No divorce, No remarriage" advocates, who work to split up people who are divorced and remarried, contend that the second marriage is not a binding marriage. They also put much stress on the word "committeth", and make it out to mean that the remarried couple are not married "In God's eyes", but only living in adultery. On this ground they won't let them in the church without separation.

It is a strange doctrine that allows a man who is a whoremonger before marriage, to finally get married. And, since it is the first marriage, he can come into the church, be accepted, and even be a bishop someday. The youth, however, who happens to marry a loser who runs off on him; but later gets married, finds the Lord, repents of his past; and comes to the church, can't even remain married. He must divorce and be single the rest of his life, whether he has the gift or not. The first person started with a lower view of marriage, because they just fornicated at first, but later got married. The second person never did fornicate, but made sure they were married both times. Yet, many say accepting the first case into the church is alright; but to accept the second case lowers the sacredness of marriage. This is simple unwillingness to consider the matter justly.

If you understand that Jesus is the Word become flesh, and did not come to change God's judgments and statutes on moral issues; but to confirm and clarify; then you will understand we must define terms and situations in the New Testament consistent with the Old Testament. If God allowed divorce and remarriage in the Old Covenant and Jesus allowed it under the same exception in the New, then a second marriage is a binding, one flesh, arrangement like the first marriage was. Now, if the first marriage was contracted sinfully, it was still a binding contract. The same holds true for the second. If a man took a second wife in the Old Testament and stopped taking care of the first, he was committing adultery against the first by not upholding the marriage covenant; but the Bible doesn't call the second marriage adultery, it just says the first is free to depart and is not bound to the first (Ex. 21:10,11). This same principle applies in the New Testament. There is nothing in the Bible that teaches that a marriage covenant is continuous adultery. Jesus is speaking consistent with the entire body of Scripture, which testifies that unlawful divorce causes the second marriage to be adulterous, but doesn't call it continued adultery and not a binding covenant.

Adultery often is an attitude of the heart, even before the act ever occurs. Jesus is primarily preaching against those who put away their wife for the *express reason* of marrying another. If your wife commits sexual sin, and you say in your heart, "O good, now I get to marry another"; then you are just as much an adulterer as she is! We are not defending you! God knows and will deal with you! We are rightly dividing God's Word to defend the poor misused and forsaken mate, who is devastated, broken hearted, and later burns for companionship. After their hopes of reconciliation are gone, and they are left to live alone for the rest of their life; we believe God allows them to find peace and rest in marriage, rather than burn with loneliness and temptation.

What about a person who divorced for the wrong reason (incompatibility, physical abuse, etc.); and then remarries while they are still under obligation to reconcile? We must consider the Law of God and what

Jesus and His apostles taught consistent with the Law of God to answer these questions. The whole transaction is adulterous and sinful; but God's Law says you are still bound in the second marriage.

Those who are Christians and know better are excommunicated and shunned when they commit known trespass against God's order. When we are dealing with people coming to the church from the world after the fact, we give them a fresh start in Christ. As quoted earlier, the early Christians believed that your life begins at conversion, and the past is past.

1. It is still an abomination to God for a person who has divorced and remarried unrighteously to ever go back to the first.

2. The second marriage (an act of adultery), breaks the obligation to reconcile (because God now forbids it). The second marriage is binding by the law, just as the first was. It is a sin to break the second marriage unlawfully, just as it was the first. When sinners repent of this; they must confess, and hate their sin; but are forgiven, and get a fresh start when they come to Christ.

Those who think they can presumptuously divorce, remarry, repent, and go on their way are sadly mistaken. God doesn't have to forgive presumptuous sin; but rather may send you strong delusion, and damn your soul (II Thess. 2:11,12). You never mock God. God's mercy is not his slavery. He will have mercy on whom he decides to have mercy; and that is on repentant followers, not those who delay repentance, so they can sin. If God brings them to repentance, then he will also forgive them, and so must we. True repentance will cause people to hate their sin more than we do.

You are not a believer, if you are not living by obedient faith in Christ to the best of your ability and maturity. We don't have to worry about this causing a low view of marriage in the church if we have biblical teaching and discipline. Those who seek unlawful divorce or commit adultery are excommunicated from a biblical church. If unlawful divorce-remarriage has happened in an unbiblical church setting, it is the same as those who are un-churched — they are living without truth. They need to repent when they come to the truth and submit to it to the best of their ability.

3. The word "committeth" is no more continuous action in the context of this passage than the word "marrieth" is. They both have the "eth", but that doesn't always mean a continuous, repeated action. According to my Hebrew/Greek Study Bible (Spiros Zodhiades); the word "committeth" is *present indicative*; of which he says, "The Present Tense in the Indicative Mood represents contemporaneous action, as opposed to action in the past or future. Other than in the indicative mood, it refers only to continuous or repeated action." The action, "committeth adultery" is contemporary with the action of "unlawful divorce and remarriage." They are not divorcing and remarrying every day, nor are they in a continual state of adultery, but guilty of the act of breaking wedlock on insufficient grounds in order to marry another.

It is erroneous to equate the word "adultery" with the word "sex". In doing this we think that as long as the man is having sexual relations, he is still committing adultery. William Tyndale's translation sheds some light on these words:

Matt. 5:31-32 "It is said, whosoever put away his wife, let him give her a testimonial also of the divorcement. But I say unto you: whosoever put away his wife, (except it be for fornication) causeth her to break matrimony. And whosoever marrieth her that is divorced, breaketh wedlock."

Matt. 19:9, "I say therefore unto you, whosoever putteth away his wife (except it be for fornication) and marrieth another, breaketh wedlock. And whosoever marrieth her which is divorced, doth commit advoutry."

Mark 10:11, "And he said unto them: Whosoever putteth away his wife and marrieth another, breaketh wedlock to her-ward. And if a woman forsake her husband and be married to another, she committeth advoutry."

Luke 16:18, "Whosoever forsaketh his wife and marrieth another, breaketh matrimony. And every man which marrieth her that is divorced from her husband, committeth advoutry also."

You can see that "break matrimony" is not a continuous act. "Break wedlock" and "advoutry" (breaking vows) is not continuous unless you keep breaking new and different vows and marriages. These words are more true to the meaning of

118

"adultery" than just "sex", **otherwise polygamy would have been adultery.**

4.   In regards to converts who come to Christ in a second marriage, we must follow the example of Jesus and the apostles. They never demanded remarried Jews to divorce before baptism, unless it was a matter of incest, homosexuality, etc. The lost of today are just as hard hearted and more ignorant than the Jews (God's covenant people) of the past. God, who didn't split up Jews and Gentiles in the first century, but forgave and took them into the church, will do the same today; when they repent and promise to never commit unlawful divorce and remarriage again.

5. Just as in other sinfully contracted marriages, they are still bound. To rebel against your parents and marry is sinful, but the marriage is still binding. To marry an unbeliever is sinful, but the marriage is still binding in the New Testament (though it wasn't in the Old Testament always).

Joshua was commanded to not make a league with the people of Canaan; but when he did, he was bound to keep it -- even in the days of Saul and David. Israel was "rejecting" God when they demanded a king; but once they did it, God held them to it. We will see in I Cor.   7 that those who come to Christ bound in a marriage are commanded, "seek not to be loosed". Look back at our comments on the woman of Samaria, whom Jesus said had 5 husbands, but the one she was now with was not her husband. Jesus didn't tell her she really had one husband and five affairs.

■ PROPER ATTITUDES

What attitudes should we have toward remarried people? If they repent and are trying to follow Jesus, does God forgive them? Can Jesus' blood cleanse them? Let me ask you another question. What attitudes should we have toward repentant drunkards and liars? Does God forgive them? Can Jesus' blood cleanse them?

Only our pride would cause us not to love, help, respect, and befriend any sinner who sincerely repents and wants to follow Jesus.

What things must you do to free yourself to remarry, if you find yourself in a divorced situation?

1. Seek forgiveness from God, your former spouse, children, relatives, and others involved.
2. Make every effort at reconciliation.
3. Make restitution wherever possible for past wrongs as:
   a. voluntary repayment of unfairly-obtained money, rights, etc. in the divorce.
   b. assuming obligations of child support, etc.
4. Be sure God doesn't want you to be single. That which you cannot do in faith is sinful. "He that doubteth is damned if he eat".

If a person has cleared himself from all obligations so that they are free to remarry; how should we feel toward them if they decide to marry? I think we need to encourage them to seek godly counsel from their pastor and parents. We shouldn't shun them or treat them as a sinner for doing what is permitted for them to do. Let us strive to have the mind of Christ on this issue. Do we want them to succeed or fail? Then we need to encourage them in the right way, not snub them and make them feel second class.

Unless people can forget those things which are behind, they cannot reach forth unto those things which are before. The Apostle Paul had to learn to forget, or he would have lived in shame and discouragement for the families he harmed before his conversion. The believers of the day didn't feel the need to remind him all the time and thus punish him; they let him go forward!

9

Before You Marry

"He that trusteth in his own heart is a fool: but whoso walketh wisely, he shall be delivered." Prov.28:26.

The disciples said to Jesus, "If the case of the man be so with his wife, it is not good to marry." Indeed, it is good to be very careful who you marry! Knowing that my life was given to the Lord to preach his Word, I tried to be very careful who I married. But, knowing my own weaknesses, I also knew I couldn't do this alone -- I needed God's help.

I was at a Christian college, away from my parents, and around many young ladies who would have been willing to court. Not being raised with a Scriptural home and church, where the parents and pastor guide the courtship and help the youth to avoid the pitfalls of choosing the wrong mate, I didn't have the safeguards I should have had. However, I did sense the danger I was in, and the importance of my future. I began to pray earnestly every day that God would not allow me to marry the wrong person.

Previous to this I had strongly considered the possibility of singleness for the Lord; but God impressed me with the need for a wife in ministerial work. As I prayed for direction, God gave me Proverbs 28:26 (above). I realized I had to keep my heart out of the decision; and use my head. I prayed for God to help me in this, and give me some practical ways to do this.

In answer to my prayer, God gave me two principles to use to keep my heart out of the decision, and be able to walk wisely:

1. When I considered the possibility of a young lady; rather than looking at her as my own future wife, I was to ask myself: "What would I tell my son (if I had one), if he asked me about marrying this girl?" Thinking of her as my son's wife kept my heart out of it, and made me think more wise and practical -- Just as a father would. I didn't have my father there to ask; but when I put myself in the father position, it helped me to think like a father. I was to ask myself, "Would I want my son to court or marry a girl such as this?"

2. The second principle God gave me was to ask myself, "Is this the kind of girl I want my daughter to be?" Most likely, if I marry this girl, my daughter will grow up like her. So, is this what I want in my daughter?...this character, this attitude, etc.

For my children, I hope they don't have to go about it like I did. I believe young people should stay with their family, not go off to college to get their MRS degree. My sons and daughters are being taught that Mother and Father are God's chosen vessels to help them to find a mate, if it is God's will. But we all will still beg God for his help, and keep our hearts out of the way, as much as is possible.

I made a list of qualities I felt I needed in a wife, being a preacher. When I met a young lady, I would rate them in these qualities from 1 - 10.

1. Responds well to authority? 1 2 3 4 5 6 7 8 9 10

2. Relationship with parents? 1 2 3 4 5 6 7 8 9 10

3. Is she a witness for Christ? 1 2 3 4 5 6 7 8 9 10

4. Relationship with God? 1 2 3 4 5 6 7 8 9 10

5. Willing to live simple? 1 2 3 4 5 6 7 8 9 10

6. Hard worker? 1 2 3 4 5 6 7 8 9 10

7. Meek & quiet, chaste? 1 2 3 4 5 6 7 8 9 10

8. Modest? 1 2 3 4 5 6 7 8 9 10

9. Agree on child discipline? 1 2 3 4 5 6 7 8 9 10

10. Agree on convictions? 1 2 3 4 5 6 7 8 9 10

.....etc.

I would recommend you do this with your parents! Work together to insure your future home and family will be a glory to Christ, and not a shame!

I thank God, because of godly leaders, I didn't kiss my wife until the wedding. We didn't hold hands until we were engaged. This builds trust and respect, which makes for lasting marriages. If a person doesn't like hands off and chaperoned courtship, then STAY AWAY FROM THEM!

■ BEFORE YOU MARRY:

1. Seek the Lord as to whether He wants you to be married; and surrender your right of marriage to Him. Become neutral in your heart about the issue, and leave it with God whether you will wed or not. This doesn't mean you shouldn't pray for God to bring someone to you, if it is his will. You should pray about it earnestly, because it is going to affect you and your children for the rest of your life, and theirs!

2. Seek the counsel of your parents, pastor, and godly brethren.

3.   Make plans with your parents for parent lead courtship. Only use "hands off", and "chaperoned" courtship. Don't pray, "lead us not into temptation", and then walk into it by choice--you are tempting God.

4. Don't court until you are old enough and mature enough to marry and raise of family. Be financially ready. Seek your parents advice.

5. I don't recommend long courtship; but just long enough to be sure of God's will.

6. Beware of marrying a divorced person. If you have kept yourself pure, then only marry someone who has

also kept himself/herself pure. Someone who has failed in past relationships is a dangerous gamble.

■ BEFORE YOU REMARRY:

1. Be sure God wants you to remarry. Make sure you have confessed and forsaken all past sin, and sought God's forgiveness for your past failures. Make sure you have made reconciliation and sought forgiveness as much as is possible with those involved in the last marriage and divorce. Make sure you have freed yourself from all previous obligations or fulfilled them (financial, child support, etc.). Make restitution as much as is possible for past wrongs.

2. Be sure you have waited long enough to be certain God doesn't want you to be single. Surrender your right to marriage. Listen to godly counsel.

3. Seek counsel concerning possible reasons why the last marriage failed, and what part you could have played in it. The fact that you were involved in a failed relationship will make it harder for you to be successful now. See what beams may be in your eye.

4. Listen to your parent's and pastor's counsel. Make sure they approve of the person before you start courting. ONLY MARRY A SPIRITUAL CHRISTIAN.

5. Make plans with your parents or pastor for chaperoned, hands off courtship. It doesn't matter how old you are, sin is still sin! You are just as vulnerable, if not more, than courting youth.

NOTE:

With fear and trembling I have prayed and approached this subject. I did not want to venture upon such a hard and life-affecting subject; but felt it my duty to do what I could. For a number of years this subject has plagued me and provoked me to study. I don't claim infallibility; but could not reconcile all the evidence with any other position consistently. Every other possible position left me with absurdities and ignored principles. I commend this study to God in faith that when I asked for bread, he did not give me a stone.

Mark Bullen is the pastor of Living Faith Christian Fellowship in Brookfield, Missouri.

For more information you are invited to visit the website at:

www.thefaithoncedelivered.info

Other Titles published by Apprehending Truth:

Heritage of Truth Books

Understanding Misunderstood Texts of Scripture
Asa Mahan, J. L. Wallace

Defining Biblical Holiness
John Wesley, Asa Mahan

The Works of John Fletcher:
Volume I: Five Checks To Antinomianism
Volume II: Creeds and Scripture Scales *(forthcoming)*
Volume III: Doctrines of Grace and Justice *(forthcoming)*
Volume IV: Portrait of Paul & An Appeal *(forthcoming)*
Volume V: A Vindication of the Faith *(forthcoming)*
Volume VI: Outlines & Miscellany *(forthcoming)*

Antinomianism and the Gospel by Aaron Carey

Apprehending Truth
*A Survey of Often Misapplied, Misappropriated,
and Misapprehended Texts and Principles of Scripture
(forthcoming)*

Deceptions of Rome *(forthcoming)*

Debating Islam *(forthcoming)*

www.publishers.apprehendingtruth.net

Buy the Truth and sell it not. ~ Proverbs xxiii, 23

Made in the USA
Charleston, SC
25 November 2012